UNDERSTANDING AND MANAGING FINANCIAL INFORMATION
The non-financial manager's guide

Michael M. Coltman, M.B.A., C.G.A.

Self-Counsel Press
(*a division of*)
International Self-Counsel Press Ltd.

Printed in Canada
First edition: September, 1993

Cataloguing in Publication Data

Coltman, Michael M. (Michael Macdonald), 1930-
    Understanding and managing financial information

    (Self-counsel business series)
    ISBN 0-88908-297-9
        1. Small business— Finance. 2. Accounting.
    I. Title. II. Series.
    HG4207.7.C64 1993   658.15′ 92   C93-091530-5

Cover photography by Andy Stokes, ATN Visuals, Vancouver, B.C.

Self-Counsel Press
(*a division of*)
International Self-Counsel Press Ltd.

1481 Charlotte Road
North Vancouver,
British Columbia V7J 1H1

1704 N. State Street
Bellingham, Washington
98225

CONTENTS

vii

SAMPLES

TABLES

1
INTRODUCTION

Entrepreneurship and small business are not new to North America. Several hundred years ago the small business operator was thriving in the form of the fur trapper and the homesteader, many of whom traded with larger companies (the monopolists of their day).

Not much has changed. Today large companies still tend to monopolize many markets, but small businesses nevertheless continue to thrive and grow by filling niches that large companies cannot handle.

a. OPPORTUNITIES FOR SMALL BUSINESS

Most businesses that are large today began as small businesses. They became large because they were well managed and took advantage of opportunities that still exist. Today, small business can start up and, given the right circumstances, can grow. Some of the opportunities that exist are the following:

(a) Trying out new ideas or products

(b) Offering personal services where the visibility and attention of the business owner is important such as in a restaurant, a beauty parlor, or an equipment repair firm

(c) Reaching a limited market, such as a grocery store that does not compete with a supermarket chain but offers necessary products when the chain stores are closed, or provides faster service since long lines at cashier stations are avoided

1

(d) Reaching a local market. A local small construction firm in a growing small town does not normally have to fear competition of the large city construction companies that need the big economies of scale to survive

(e) Catering to seasonal demands by being able to quickly adjust production to changing demands. Large manufacturing companies, for example, cannot retool quickly in the short run. They need large, stable markets and the manufacture of large quantities of products in order to remain profitable.

1. Adaptability of small business

Large corporations, because of their size and financial power, are frequently able to avoid the competition that small businesses face. A small business survives because it is much more adaptable and, therefore, more efficient than a huge corporate enterprise. Decision making is immediate and effective in a small business but slow, cumbersome, and often irrational in a large conglomerate where committees, rather than a down-to-earth sense or feeling about the market place, dictate decisions.

This adaptability is illustrated by the employment record of small businesses in the past 10 years. During this period an estimated 5 million new firms have been started (unfortunately not all of them have survived), and they have provided approximately 85% of all new jobs created. At the same time employment in larger firms, many of them in manufacturing, has declined, as these firms reacted slowly to the changing demand for their products and have been less able to compete with foreign manufacturers.

b. SMALL BUSINESS DEFINITION

What is a small business? Definitions abound, but many of them are meaningless, particularly when expressed in terms of annual sales dollars or number of persons employed. Perhaps the best description is that which defines a small business as one that is independently owned and operated and not dominant in its field.

It is estimated that there are more than 11.5 million non-farm businesses (out of about 12 million in total) in North America that fit this definition. Most of them are labor intensive and provide employment opportunities far in excess of their relative size.

Most of these small companies were established to manufacture, distribute, and retail a variety of goods and services. Even though the large corporations receive much publicity, most of them are dependent on small business. For example, companies that mass produce manufactured goods could not possibly distribute them without the myriad of small firms that handle transportation, wholesaling, and retailing. In other words, small business enterprises constitute the backbone of free enterprise economies.

c. SKILLS REQUIRED

Traditionally, the level of management skills has been considerably less in small businesses than in larger ones, but the market that these small businesses face is just as complex as that to which large corporations are exposed.

The small business entrepreneur needs basically the same management skills as managers in large business. They both must plan, make decisions based on the best information available, and prepare strategies for the future. The small business owner/manager must make constant decisions to solve problems, establish priorities, determine policies, make financial decisions, and so on. In addition, operating results must be constantly analyzed, and outside factors that may have an effect on the internal operations of the business must be considered.

The individual small business owner must, however, assume a wider range of responsibilities than the general manager of a large corporation. The manager of a large corporation will have vice-presidents of finance, marketing, manufacturing and production, distribution, and so on. Each of these vice-presidents has important responsibilities, but each is concerned with only one specific area of the company's activities.

In the small business, the owner generally has a daily responsibility for all of the above as well as for ongoing problems concerning personnel, inventory, sales, credit, suppliers, new policy implementation, new product introductions, public relations, marketing, and financial reporting.

However, it is difficult for the small business entrepreneur to copy the skills required for large businesses since these skills need to be adapted and scaled down. Unfortunately, most of the books and material written to help businesses and managers survive are written for the large, corporation enterprise. This one is not.

d. RISK INVOLVED

Those who go into small business do so in spite of, or in ignorance of, the skills required and the odds for survival. A rule of thumb for new small businesses is that 50% fail during the first year, and 90% fail in less than five years.

Statistical analysis of business failures in North America shows that the following causes make up more than 95% of the failures:

(a) Lack of competence to run the business

(b) Lack of experience in that type of business

(c) Lack of managerial experience

(d) Unbalanced experience

In addition, small business failures are said to be caused by any of all of the following specific problems:

(a) Inability to find competent employees

(b) Inadequate starting capital

(c) Inability to finance expansion

(d) Inadequate sales because of lack of demand for the product or service

(e) High operating expenses

(f) Limited credit from suppliers

(g) Shortage of working capital

(h) Poor location

(i) Inability to make a new product known to the market

(j) Impossible tax burdens

(k) Failure to formulate and plan objectives

(l) Pressure from large competitors with a vested interest to see the business fail

(m) Inability to keep proper accounting records

You will notice that many of the items mentioned in the above list relate to financial factors. In fact, most aspects of a business are eventually reflected in one way or another in the financial statements. The small business owner's ability to interpret, analyze, and make decisions about the information presented by the financial statements and related financial information is what this book is all about.

2
AN OVERVIEW OF ACCOUNTING

Owners of small businesses often react to accounting in horror, with visions of spending "accountless" hours on journals, ledgers and other mysterious accounting records. Because of the apparent mystery surrounding accounting, many small firm owners fail to keep adequate records and make no attempt to understand the basics of accounting. As a result, they often do not know whether the business made a profit or a loss until weeks after the end of their fiscal year simply because their accountant has not had time to prepare proper financial statements.

Although "official" financial statements are important and necessary in matters such as filing income tax returns, there is no reason why the owner of any small business, given adequate accounting records, cannot prepare interim financial statements that will give at least some indication of how the business is faring on an annual, or preferably, a monthly basis.

You don't have to be an accountant to do this. (And your accountant wouldn't want you to be one since he or she wants to stay in business too.) All you need is a basic understanding of the process and language of accounting. With this and the help of your accountant to set up some simple accounting records, you can do much of the basic bookkeeping work yourself and even prepare preliminary financial statements.

a. BASIC ACCOUNTING INFORMATION

Any business needs to have a record of some basic information.

1. Sales

Sales (sometimes called revenue) should be recorded by the day, week, month, or quarter, then further broken down into cash or credit (by type of credit card if necessary), and by department, type of merchandise, or kind of product.

Credit sales are necessary to determine the amount of accounts receivable (money owed to you) at any particular time. Electronic registers can readily provide much of the required detail concerning sales without requiring extensive paperwork.

2. Operating expenses

Operating expenses should be recorded by type (e.g., purchases, supplies, rent) in total by sales period, and even by department, or type of merchandise or product. In a manufacturing company, expenses are often broken down into departments such as manufacturing, selling, and administration. In addition, unpaid expenses at any time need to be known since these form your accounts payable.

3. Payroll

This is a major expense for most firms and one that has legal requirements concerning the detail that you must record. In particular, payroll withholdings for taxes and other required deductions must be properly documented.

4. Inventory

Inventory should be taken at least annually and, in certain businesses, as frequently as monthly. Inventory must be separated by type, and even by item. Electronic sales registers can often be used to record reductions in inventory as a result of a sale.

For all sales and expenses it is important that you keep all documents supporting any transactions such as sales slips, register tapes, or invoices; purchase invoices and/or receiving reports; canceled checks for both operating expenses and payroll; and receipt or memos for cash payouts not otherwise supported by an invoice or check.

b. THE BALANCE SHEET EQUATION

Accounting was developed to identify and record financial information about a business. It provides information about your company's assets and debts, your investment, sales (revenue), and expenses. It permits you or your accountant to prepare, in addition to the basic financial statements (balance sheet and income statement), other financial reports and analyses that will help you make decisions and run an efficient, effective business.

In every business, a set of financial statements is prepared periodically to monitor the progress of the business. The basic documents in this set of financial statements are an income statement and a balance sheet — both of which are discussed in more detail in the next chapter.

The income statement shows the revenues (sales) less the expenses to arrive at net income. The net income (or loss, if expenses exceed revenues) is transferred to the balance sheet and becomes part of the owner's equity. If all entries for transactions have been made correctly, the balance sheet will then "balance." The balance sheet equation is the following: Assets = liabilities + owners' equity.

Assets are things owned by your business (e.g., cash, inventory, building). Liabilities are items owed by your business (e.g., debts or obligations, including unpaid accounts, bank loans, or a mortgage on the building).

Owners' equity (also sometimes referred to as "net worth") is the difference between the assets and the liabilities. It is comprised of the money that you and any other owners have invested in the business, plus the profits of the business, less any losses, since the business began.

It perhaps makes more sense, from an owner's perspective, to state the balance sheet equation as: Assets - liabilities = owners' equity. That would be the case if the business were sold or liquidated. In other words, the assets would be sold off, the liabilities paid off, and the owner(s) would receive whatever was left. However, logical as this view of the balance sheet is, accountants prefer to express the equation in the traditional way since an even "balance" is then maintained.

c. TRANSACTION

A business transaction is an exchange of goods or services (e.g., the sale of an item in a retail store). In accounting, each transaction affects two or more accounts. This is why it is frequently referred to as double-entry accounting. No transaction can affect only one account. In this way, the balance sheet is always kept in balance and your accountant is eternally happy. Every transaction causes increases and/or decreases in asset and/or liability and/or owners' equity accounts.

This is illustrated very simply. Suppose you start a new retail business by investing $25,000 of your own savings in shares of the new company. The balance sheet would look like this:

ASSETS		OWNER'S EQUITY	
Cash:	$25,000	Shares:	$25,000

Then you purchase $5,000 of goods on credit from a wholesaler so that you will have an inventory of goods on hand to sell in your retail store. The balance sheet (again, assets = liabilities + owner's equity) would now look like this:

ASSETS		LIABILITY	
Cash:	$25,000	Accounts payable:	$ 5,000
Inventory:	$ 5,000		
		OWNER'S EQUITY	
		Shares	$25,000
TOTALS:	$30,000		$30,000

9

The balance sheet still balances since the left-hand side (totalling $30,000) equals the right-hand side (also totalling $30,000). In normal practice, transactions like this are not recorded directly onto the balance sheet (since the balance sheet just wouldn't have enough room on it). They are entered into accounting records called journals and then into accounts in a ledger, or directly into the accounts in the ledger. It is the ledger, supported by the journals, that is commonly called the "books of account."

d. ACCOUNTS

There is usually one account in the ledger for each type of asset, liability, owners' equity, sale (revenue), and expense. At the end of each accounting period, only the account balances at that time are transferred either to the balance sheet or to the income statement. The income statement details all the income and expense accounts that comprise the owners' equity account on the balance sheet.

In accounting, each account is considered to have a left-hand side and a right-hand side. The left-hand side is where debit (usually abbreviated to DDr) entries are made, and the right-hand side is where credit (Cr) entries are made:

Debit (Dr)	Credit (Cr)

Because of their shape, these accounts are referred to as "T" accounts. In practice, you will never see accounts that look like this but they are a very useful learning device.

Account pages in ledgers are a bit more sophisticated; nevertheless, even with computer-produced accounts and financial statements, the same basic principle of debits and credits applies.

When you enter transactions in the accounts, make sure the entries in the debit side of the accounts always equal the entries in the credit side. If you don't, the balance sheet will not balance. At the end of each accounting period, as the accounts are closed, the difference between the debit and credit entries provides the balance figure for each account.

It is wrong to view debits as increases and credits as decreases in the balance of accounts. Debits or credits can either increase or decrease the balance. These rules are illustrated in the following "T" accounts:

ASSETS		=	LIABILITIES		+	OWNERS' EQUITY	
Debits	Credits		Debits	Credits		Debits	Credits
increase	decrease		decrease	increase		decrease	increase
balance	balance		balance	balance		balance	balance

Since sales revenue (income) increases owners' equity, sales account entries have the same effect as those for the owners' equity account, and since expenses decrease owners' equity, expense account entries are the reverse of those for sales. This is illustrated by the following:

SALES		EXPENSES	
Debits	Credits	Debits	Credits
decrease	increase	increase	decrease
balance	balance	balance	balance

11

The normal account balance for each of the five types of accounts would be:

ACCOUNT	NORMAL BALANCE
Assets	Debit
Liabilities	Credit
Owners' equity	Credit
Sales	Credit
Expenses	Debit

and an example of each would be:

Asset:

Cash	
12,000	

Liability:

Accounts Payable	
	5,000

Owners' equity:

Shares	
	8,000

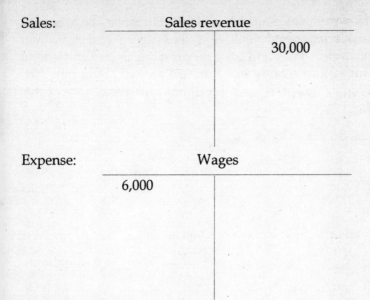

Sales:	Sales revenue	
		30,000

Expense:	Wages	
6,000		

e. MATCHING PRINCIPLE

An important concept in accounting is the matching principle. The matching principle states that transactions are recorded at the time they occur and not necessarily at the time cash is exchanged. In other words, a regular customer may be allowed to charge a purchase to an account that is sent after the end of the month. Under the matching principle, the sale would be shown as revenue for the month even though the cash may not be received for another month.

This matching is known as accrual accounting, as opposed to cash accounting under which entries are made in the books only when cash is received or given out.

This does not suggest that cash basis accounting should never be used. In fact, it might be quite a good idea to use it. For example, a small business that sells on a cash only basis and that pays cash for wages and supplies might well use a cash basis accounting system, or a combination cash/accrual system.

However, since most established businesses have at least some purchases and sales, as well as other transactions that are not a cash basis, and since for most businesses, the federal tax authorities require that you use accrual accounting, the matching concept is used throughout the remainder of this book.

3
FINANCIAL STATEMENTS

It is not necessary to be able to prepare financial statements to understand them. However, if you have some idea how to put together financial statements (an income statement and a balance sheet), you may have the advantage of being able to analyze the information in greater depth.

The two major components in a set of financial statements are the balance sheet and the income statement. The following sections about the balance sheet and the income statement should be read and analyzed jointly. The important relationship between the two is clear when you compare the definitions of the two types of statement:

(a) The balance sheet gives a picture of the financial position of a business at a particular point in time

(b) The income statement shows the operating results of the business over a period of time

The period of time referred to for the income statement usually ends on the date of the balance sheet.

a. THE BALANCE SHEET

As was stated above, the balance sheet gives a picture of the financial condition of a business at a particular point in time. On the left-hand or debit side, it lists the assets or resources that a business has. On the right-hand or credit side it lists liabilities (or debts of the company) and the stockholders' equity. On a balance sheet, total assets always equal total liabilities plus equity (this is the balance sheet equation discussed in chapter 2).

15

The assets side of the balance sheet is generally broken down into three sections: current assets, fixed or long-term assets, and other assets. The breakdown of assets into these sections is not for balancing reasons, but for the convenience of the firm's owners and other readers of the financial statements.

1. Current assets

Current assets are cash or items that can or will be converted into cash within a short period of time (usually a year or less).

Current assets include items such as cash on hand, cash in the bank, marketable securities (e.g., term deposits into which temporary surplus cash has been invested), accounts receivable, inventories, and prepaid expenses (e.g., insurance, property tax, and similar items that have been paid in advance but not "used up" at the balance sheet date).

2. Fixed (long-term) assets

Fixed or long-term assets are those of a relatively permanent nature, not intended for sale, that are used in generating revenue. For example, this category of assets would include the land, building, fixtures, and equipment (including automotive equipment such as delivery trucks) that are owned by the business.

These items are shown on the balance sheet at their cost. The accumulated depreciation is deducted from the cost. Accumulated depreciation is the estimated decline in value of the assets due to wear and tear, the passage of time, changed economic conditions or other factors. (Depreciation will be discussed in more detail in the next chapter.)

The difference between the asset cost figure and the accumulated depreciation is referred to as *net book value*. Net book value does not necessarily reflect the current market or replacement value of the assets in question.

3. Other assets

If a business has any other assets that do not fit into either the current or fixed categories, they are included here. An example might be leasehold costs or improvements. For example, if improvements are made to a building that you are leasing, they benefit the business for the remaining life of the lease. The costs should be spread over this life.

This cost spread is much like depreciation, except that in cases such as leasehold property it is generally called amortization.

Another example would be goodwill. Goodwill is the price you pay in excess of the value of the tangible assets (land, building, equipment) when you purchase an existing business.

4. Total assets

The total of all the asset figures (current, fixed, and other) gives the total asset value, or total resources, of the business.

5. Liabilities and owners' equity

On the right-hand side of the balance sheet are the liabilities and owners' equity sections. The liabilities and equity side of the balance sheet shows how the assets have been financed or paid for. The liability section has two parts: current liabilities and long-term liabilities.

(a) Current liabilities

Current liabilities are those debts that must be paid, or are expected to be paid, in less than a year.

Current liabilities include items such as accounts payable (e.g., for purchases of supplies), accrued expenses (e.g., wages/salaries due to employees, payroll tax deductions, and similar items), income tax payable, and the portion of any long-term loans or mortgages that are due within the next year.

(b) Long-term liabilities

Long-term liabilities are the debts of the business that are payable more than one year after the balance sheet date. Included in this category would be mortgages and any similar long-term loans.

6. Owners' equity

In general terms, the owners' equity section of the balance sheet is the difference between the total assets and the total liabilities. It represents the equity, or the net worth, of the owner(s) of the business.

If you are operating your own business it is likely that it will be established as a limited or incorporated company. In an incorporated company the owners' equity is comprised of two main items: capital (shares) and retained earnings.

An incorporated company is limited to a maximum number of shares it can issue. This limit is known as the authorized number of shares. Shares generally have a par, or stated, value. It is this par value, multiplied by the number of shares actually issued up to the authorized quantity, that gives the total value of capital on the balance sheet.

Most small businesses that operate as incorporated companies issue "common shares." However, some also issue "preferred shares." Preferred shares rank ahead of common shares, up to certain limits, as far as dividends are concerned. Preferred stockholders may have special voting rights, and they rank ahead of common stockholders if the business is liquidated.

The other part of the owners' equity section of the balance sheet is retained earnings. Retained earnings links the income statement and the balance sheet. For that reason the retained earnings part of the owners' equity section of the balance sheet is discussed below, after you have had a chance to read about the income statement.

A balance sheet is illustrated in Sample #1.

b. THE INCOME STATEMENT

The income statement shows the operating results of the business for a period of time (month, quarter, half-year, or year). Formal income statements are prepared at least once a year (this is required for income tax filing reasons, if for no other) and informal ones more frequently.

The income statement shows income from sales (revenue) less any expenses made to achieve that revenue. An income statement for a service firm (a travel agent) is illustrated in Sample #2. A similar type of income statement would be prepared for other types of service firms, such as laundries (see Sample #3), consulting firms, and repair companies.

The amount of detail concerning revenue and expenses to be shown on the income statement depends on the type and size of the business and the needs of the owner/operator for more or less information.

In a manufacturing or wholesale company, and in some types of retail firms, the income statement would include a cost of goods sold section that is deducted from revenue to produce a gross margin or gross profit figure before other expenses are deducted. The reason for this is that the cost of goods sold figure and the gross profit to sales figure (expressed as a percentage of the related sales) are important benchmarks for measuring the success of the business. Sample #4 illustrates how cost of goods sold and gross profit are presented on an income statement.

One of the major items of expense that appears on most income statements is depreciation. Since depreciation is a special kind of expense, it is discussed separately in the next chapter.

c. RETAINED EARNINGS

Usually the balance sheet and the income statement are accompanied by a statement of retained earnings. The statement of retained earnings is the place where the net profit of the business (from the income statement) for a period of time (let us say a year) is added to the preceding year's figure of retained earnings to give the new total. In other words, the retained earnings are the accumulated net profits, less any losses, sustained by the business since it began.

The retained earnings are not necessarily represented by cash in the bank because the money may have been used for other necessary purposes such as purchasing new equipment or physically expanding the size of the building.

A completed statement of retained earnings is illustrated in Sample #5. Note how the $66,000 net profit from the income statement (Sample #4) has been transferred to the statement of retained earnings (Sample #5) and the year-end retained earnings figure of $229,000 transferred to the balance sheet (Sample #1).

SAMPLE #1
BALANCE SHEET

MASTERPIECE MANUFACTURING LTD. — Balance Sheet as at June 30, 199-

ASSETS

Current Assets

Cash		$ 28,000
Accounts receivable		43,000
Marketable securities		10,000
Inventories		146,000
Prepaid expenses		5,000
Total current assets		$232,000

Fixed Assets

Land, at cost			$92,000
Building, at cost	$1,333,000		
Less: Accumulated depreciation	57,000	976,000	
Equipment, at cost	$374,000		
Less: Accumulated depreciation	275,000	99,000	
Total fixed assets			1,167,000

Other Assets

Deferred expense		6,000
Total Assets		$1,405,000

LIABILITIES & OWNERS' EQUITY

Current Liabilities

Accounts payable		$ 19,000
Accrued expenses		4,000
Income tax payable		13,000
Current portion of mortgage		27,000
Total current liabilities		$63,000

Long-Term Liabilities

Mortgage on building	$840,000	
Less: current portion	27,000	813,000
Total Liabilities		$876,000

Owners' Equity

Capital — authorized 5,000 common shares @ $100 par value; issued and outstanding 3,000 shares	$300,000	
Retained earnings	229,000	529,000
Total Liabilities & Equity		$1,405,000

21

SAMPLE #2
INCOME STATEMENT — SERVICE BUSINESS

SUNSATIONAL TRAVEL LTD.

Income Statement for Year Ending December 31, 199-

Operating revenues		$2,100,000
Payments to carriers and suppliers		1,900,000
Net commission income		$200,000
Operating expenses:		
Salaries and wages	$120,000	
Selling-related costs	32,000	
Administration costs	22,000	
Rent and other	11,000	185,000
Profit before tax		$15,000
Income tax		6,000
Net profit		$9,000

IMMACULATE CLEANING COMPANY

Income Statement for Year Ending December 31, 199-

Sales:

Laundry	$135,000	
Dry cleaning	45,000	
Repairs and sundry	10,000	$190,000

Operating expenses:

Salaries and wages	$94,000	
Operating and supplies	22,000	
Repairs and miscellaneous	4,000	
Accounting and legal	2,000	
Advertising	2,000	
Sundry	4,000	128,000
Profit before overheads		$ 62,000

Overhead expenses:

Rent	$12,000	
Utilities	6,000	
Insurance	3,000	
Taxes and licenses	3,000	
Depreciation — equipment	10,000	34,000
Profit before tax		$ 28,000
Income tax		7,000
Net profit		$ 21,000

SAMPLE #4
INCOME STATEMENT — MANUFACTURING BUSINESS

MASTERPIECE MANUFACTURING Income Statement for Year Ending June 30, 199-	
Sales	$1,250,000
Cost of goods sold	450,000
Gross profit	$ 800,000
Operating expenses: (listed in detail)	668,000
Profit before income tax	$ 132,000
Income tax	66,000
Net profit	$ 66,000

SAMPLE #5
STATEMENT OF RETAINED EARNINGS

MASTERPIECE MANUFACTURING Statement of Retained Earnings for Year Ending June 30, 199-	
Retained earnings beginning of year	$193,000
Add profit for year	66,000
	$259,000
Deduct dividends paid	30,000
Retained earnings June 30, 199-	$229,000

4
DEPRECIATION

When Billy Big purchased a new building for his business, he recorded it on his balance sheet as long-life asset at its original cost price. In each accounting period that benefits from the use of the new building, Billy records a portion of the cost on the income statement. At the same time he deducts from the balance sheet by way of accumulated depreciation. (See chapter 3.)

This portion of cost on Billy's income statement is called depreciation. It is shown as an expense and reduces net income for that period. This immediately improves Billy's cash flow since depreciation is non-cash expense. That is, it does not require an outlay of cash at the time Billy records the depreciation expense. It simply reduces on the books the value of the related asset.

This means Billy is reducing taxable profits and saving on income tax, which means he also saves cash or increases cash flow.

Most businesses, like Billy's, will claim the maximum depreciation possible for tax purposes. What is the useful life of an asset for depreciation purposes? This is a matter of opinion influenced by factors such as inadequacy, obsolescence, and economic changes. In the case of a building, useful life could be 30, 40, or 50 years or more. In the case of a piece of equipment, it could be as short as a couple of years if a new and better piece of equipment becomes available.

There are a number of different methods for calculating depreciation, such as straight-line, declining balance, and units of production.

a. STRAIGHT-LINE DEPRECIATION

The straight-line method is probably the simplest of all depreciation methods because it spreads the cost of the asset, less any estimated trade-in or scrap value, equally over each year of the life of the asset. The equation for calculating the annual amount of depreciation is —

$$\frac{\text{Cost of asset - Trade-in value}}{\text{Service life of asset in years}}$$

If Billy Big purchases a piece of equipment at an initial cost of $32,000 and with a trade-in value of $2,000 at the end of its five-year life, the annual depreciation will be:

$$\frac{\$32,000 - \$2,000}{5 \text{ years}} \qquad \frac{\$30,000}{5} \qquad = \$6,000 \text{ per year}$$

To obtain the monthly depreciation expense, Billy would simply divide the annual rate by 12.

Under the straight-line method, with a five-year life, one-fifth (or 20%) of the cost of the asset less its trade-in value was the annual depreciation.

b. DECLINING BALANCE DEPRECIATION

Using the same facts as above under the declining balance method, the straight-line depreciation rate of 20% is doubled to 40%. This 40% is multiplied by the undepreciated balance (book value) of the asset each year to obtain the depreciation expense for that year. Under this method, any trade-in or scrap value is ignored.

In other words, in year one, the depreciation expense would be 40% x $32,000 (the cost of the asset) = $12,800. The book value of the asset is now $32,000 - $12,800 = $19,200. Year two depreciation expense is 40% x $19,200 = $7,680. If this information is set up in the form of a schedule for all five years it would appear as follows:

YEAR	ANNUAL DEPRECIATION				NET BOOK VALUE
					$32,000
1	40% x	$32,000	=	$12,800	19,200
2	40 x	19,200	=	7,680	11,520
3	40 x	11,520	=	4,608	6,912
4	40 x	6,912	=	2,765	4,147
5	40 x	4,147	=	1,659	2,488

The declining balance method of depreciation is sometimes referred to as an accelerated method. You will note that the depreciation expense is high in the early years and decreases as the years go by. The philosophy of this accelerated method is that in the earlier years of the life of an asset maintenance costs are low, but increase with age. Therefore, in theory, the sum of depreciation plus maintenance should be approximately the same each year.

There are also tax advantages to using accelerated depreciation. Since depreciation is higher in the early years and can be claimed as an expense, the taxable profit will be lower and income taxes reduced. Over the long run, the total tax will be the same, but, by reducing income taxes in the early years, cash flow can be increased in early years which are often crucial for a new small business.

c. UNITS OF PRODUCTION DEPRECIATION

The equation for the units of production depreciation method is —

$$\frac{\text{Cost of asset - Trade in value}}{\text{Estimated units of production during life of asset}}$$

27

Sally Small purchased an item of equipment for $8,000. She estimates that this equipment will produce 50,000 items before it is traded in for $800 at the end of its useful life. The cost of depreciation per unit of production will be —

$$\frac{\$8,000 - \$800}{50,000} = \frac{\$7,200}{50,000} = \$0.144$$

Annual depreciation expense is then based on the units produced in that year. Sally assumes that 10,000 units will be produced in year one, so the annual depreciation would be 10,000 x $0.144 = $1,440. Subsequent years' depreciation would be calculated in a similar manner.

The units of production method of depreciation does have the advantage of equitably spreading total depreciation over each period of the asset's useful life. However, it does not easily allow calculation of each period's depreciation expense in advance (e.g., in budgeting, to be covered in chapter 11). Nor is it likely to give higher depreciation amounts in the early years of the asset's life which, as mentioned earlier, is useful for reducing income taxes and increasing cash flow.

d. WHICH DEPRECIATION METHOD SHOULD YOU USE?

The choice of depreciation method to use is sometimes a difficult decision for the small business entrepreneur. Regardless of the method selected, you must remember one thing: you can never record more depreciation for an asset than the cost of that asset.

Whether the asset is depreciated by an accelerated method or not, total depreciation expense cannot exceed the investment in that asset. Generally speaking, it is wise to show on the income statement the maximum depreciation that can be claimed to minimize income tax.

This does not mean that you cannot use a different method, or different rate of depreciation, on your books.

However, when you file your annual tax return, you cannot deduct on your income statement for tax reduction purposes any depreciation in excess of the allowable rates. Also, note that you can't ever claim any depreciation on land that your company owns. Land is a nondepreciable asset as far as the tax authorities are concerned.

Since this subject can be quite complex, and the regulations concerning it are changed by the government from time to time, it is best to consult with your accountant in any matter concerning depreciation. This is particularly true if you are buying the assets of a business from another company and you wish to maximize the total depreciation that you can claim in future years on those purchased assets.

5

INCOME STATEMENT ANALYSIS

In an earlier chapter, you saw examples of income statements expressed in dollars, which can provide useful information for a small business owner/operator when monitoring the progress of the business's operations, particularly if the statements are produced on a monthly basis.

a. COMMON SIZE STATEMENTS

Sometimes it is useful to convert the dollar information on income statements to "common size." Common size simply means that the dollars are converted to a percentage basis. Total sales are usually given the value of 100%, and all other items are expressed in ratio form to that 100%. Sample #6 illustrates an income statement converted to a common size basis.

The net profit, expressed as a percent of sales, is calculated by dividing net profit by sales and multiplying by 100:

$$\frac{\$\,21,000}{\$190,000} \times 100 = 11.1\%$$

Each item on the statement can be converted in the same way by dividing it by total sales and multiplying by 100.

However, an acceptable profit to sales ratio (such as that just calculated) does not mean that the income statement should not have further analysis. In chapter 6, we look at some of the ways of further analyzing income statement information with the balance sheet.

1. Comparative common size income statements

An individual income statement is often not very meaningful by itself. Two or more successive income statements compared to each other, and preferably on a common size basis, are more valuable. For example, Sample #7 illustrates an income statement placed alongside the income statement for the preceding year, with each of them expressed in common size (or percentage) terms.

In this way, changes from one year to the next are more apparent. Whether you prepare your own income statements or have your accountant do this, it is invariably a good idea to compare the current period's income statement with the previous period's.

By converting dollar amounts to percentages, you make comparison a lot easier. For example, Sample #7 shows the net profit was $21,000 in year 1 and $25,000 in year 2. Total sales increased from $190,000 to $206,000.

In relative terms, has the profit gone up at a faster or slower rate than sales? This is not easy to tell by looking only at the dollar figures. But by converting the net profit to a percentage of sales we see that it has gone from 11.1% of sales in year 1 to 12.1% of sales in year 2. In other words, in the second year, we managed to obtain a larger proportion of sales as net profit, and that is desirable.

b. TREND RESULTS

Limiting an analysis to only two period (weeks, months, or years) can be misleading if an unusual occurrence or factor distorted the results for either of the two periods. Looking at results over a greater number of periods can often be more useful in indicating the direction in which your business is heading. For example, consider trend results for a business for six successive months:

SAMPLE #6
COMMON SIZE INCOME STATEMENT

IMMACULATE CLEANING COMPANY
Common Size Income Statement for Year Ending December 31, 199-

Sales:			
Laundry	$135,000		71.0%
Dry cleaning	45,000		23.7
Repairs and sundry	10,000		5.3
		$190,000	100.0%
Operating expenses:			
Salaries and wages	$ 94,000		49.5%
Operating supplies	22,000		11.6
Repairs and miscellaneous	4,000		2.1
Accounting and legal	2,000		1.0
Advertising	2,000		1.0
Sundry	4,000		2.1
		128,000	67.3
Profit before overheads		$ 62,000	32.7%
Overhead expenses:			
Rent	$ 12,000		6.3%
Utilities	6,000		3.2
Insurance	3,000		1.6
Taxes and licenses	3,000		1.6
Depreciation — equipment	10,000		5.2
	34,000		17.9
Profit before tax	$ 28,000		14.8%
Income tax	7,000		3.7
Net profit	$ 21,000		11.1%

32

SAMPLE #7
COMPARATIVE COMMON SIZE INCOME STATEMENTS

	For Years Ending December 31, 199- and December 31, 199-			
	Year 1		Year 2	
Sales:				
Laundry	$135,000	71.0%	$148,000	71.9%
Dry cleaning	45,000	23.7	47,000	22.8
Repairs and sundry	10,000	5.3	11,000	5.3
	$190,000	100.0%	$206,000	100.0%
Operating expenses:				
Salaries and wages	$ 94,000	49.5%	$ 99,000	48.1%
Operating supplies	22,000	11.6	24,000	11.7
Repairs and misc.	4,000	2.1	5,000	2.4
Accounting and legal	2,000	1.0	2,000	1.0
Advertising	2,000	1.0	2,000	1.0
Sundry	4,000	2.1	5,000	2.4
	128,000	67.3	137,000	66.6
Profit before overheads	$ 62,000	32.7%	$ 69,000	33.4%
Overhead expenses:				
Rent	$ 12,000	6.3%	$ 14,000	6.8%
Utilities	6,000	3.2	7,000	3.4
Insurance	3,000	1.6	3,000	1.4
Taxes and licenses	3,000	1.6	3,000	1.4
Depreciation—equipment	10,000	5.2	8,000	3.9
	34,000	17.9	35,000	16.9
Profit before tax	$ 28,000	14.8%	$34,000	16.5%
Income tax	7,000	3.7	9,000	4.4
Net profit	$ 21,000	11.1%	$ 25,000	12.1%

MONTH	SALES	CHANGE IN SALES	PERCENTAGE CHANGE
1	$25,000		
2	30,000	+ $5,000	+ 20%
3	33,000	+ 3,000	+ 10
4	35,000	+ 2,000	+ 6
5	36,000	+ 1,000	+ 3
6	36,000	+ 0	+ 0

In the above figures, the change in sales dollar amounts for each period is calculated by subtracting from each month's sales the sales of the preceding month. For example, in month 3:

$33,000 - $30,000 = $3,000 change in sales

The percentage change figures are calculated by dividing each period's change in sales amount by the sales of the previous period and multiplying by 100. For example, in month 3:

$$\frac{\$3,000}{\$30,000} \times 100 = 10\%$$

Over a long enough period of time, trend results show the direction the business is going. In this particular case, the trend results indicate that although business has been increasing over the past few months, it now seems to have leveled off. Has the business reached its maximum potential in sales? Trend information such as this is useful in forecasting or budgeting (as we shall see in chapter 11).

c. INDEX TRENDS

An index trend is a way of looking at trends by first converting the dollar amounts to an index. An index is calculated by assigning a value of 100 (or 100%) in period one (the base period) for each item being tabulated. The index figure for each succeeding period is calculated by dividing the dollar amount for that period by the base period dollar amount and multiplying by 100.

The sales and wages cost dollar amounts in Table #1 have each been converted to an index trend. For example, in period 2 the sales index is —

$$\frac{\$30,000}{\$25,000} \times 100 = 120$$

In period 4 the wage cost index is

$$\frac{\$10,800}{\$7,500} \times 100 = 144$$

The completed index trend results in this particular case show that the wage cost has been increasing faster than sales. Expressed another way, sales are up 44% (144 - 100) and wage cost is up 49% (149 - 100). This is normally an undesirable trend that needs investigation and possible correction.

TABLE #1
TREND INDEX

Period	Sales	Wage Cost	Sales Index	Wages Cost Index
1	$25,000	$7,500	100	100
2	$30,000	$9,200	120	123
3	$33,000	$10,300	132	137
4	$35,000	$10,800	140	144
5	$36,000	$11,100	144	148
6	$36,000	$11,200	144	149

d. ADJUSTING FOR INFLATION

When comparing operating results and analyzing trend figures, you must be aware of the effect of changing dollar values on the results. One hundred pounds of raw materials for a manufacturing company a few years ago weighed exactly the same as one hundred pounds of raw materials today; but the amount of money required to buy those one hundred pounds today is probably quite different from the amount needed a few years ago. Prices change over time. Therefore, when you compare income and expense items over a period of time, you must consider the implications of inflation.

Consider a small business with $200,000 of sales in year one and $210,000 in year two. This is a $10,000 or 5% increase in sales. But if sales prices have been increased over the year by 10% due to inflation, then the second year sales should have been $220,000 just to stay even.

In other words, when comparing sales for successive periods in inflationary times, you are comparing unequal values. Last year's dollar does not have the same value as this year's. But there is a method that will allow you to convert a previous period's dollars into current period dollars so that your trends can be analyzed more meaningfully.

e. THE CONSUMER PRICE INDEX

The consumer price index (CPI) is probably one of the most commonly used and widely understood indexes available. But many other indexes are produced by the government and other organizations. If you select the appropriate index, dollar conversion is simple. Consider the following, which shows trend results for a small business's sales for the past five years.

Tom Trendy wanted to compare the sales figures of the small business that he had owned and operated for five years. First, he wrote down all the information to give him the trend results.

36

YEAR	SALES	CHANGE IN SALES	PERCENTAGE CHANGE
1	$420,000	0	0
2	450,000	$30,000	7.1%
3	465,000	15,000	3.3
4	485,000	20,000	4.3
5	510,000	25,000	5.2

Tom saw that he had an increase in sales each year — generally a favorable trend. But he knew he couldn't reasonably compare $420,000 of sales in year 1 with $510,000 of sales in year 5.

By selecting an appropriate index (such as the consumer price index) and adjusting all sales to comparable year 5 dollar values, Tom had a more realistic picture of the business's sales. Tom used an index that was based on the same period of time for which he wished to adjust his sales (or expenses). The index numbers were as follows:

YEAR	INDEX NUMBER
1	105
2	112
3	119
4	128
5	142

Then Tom converted the past period's (historic) dollars to current (real) dollars with the following equation:

$$\text{Historic dollars} \times \frac{\text{Index number for current period}}{\text{Index number for historic period}} = \text{Current dollars}$$

Now Tom can see the sales dollar information converted by the index numbers to express the five-year sales in terms of today's current dollars. (See Table #2.)

The resulting picture is quite different from the unadjusted historic figures. In fact, Tom's annual sales have generally declined from year 1 to year 5, which is not normally a desirable trend.

TABLE #2
HISTORIC SALES CONVERTED TO CURRENT DOLLARS

Year	Index	Historic Sales	x	Conversion Equation	=	Current Dollars
1	105	$420,000	x	142/105	=	$568,000
2	112	450,000	x	142/112	=	571,000
3	119	465,000	x	142/119	=	555,000
4	128	485,000	x	142/128	=	538,000
5	142	510,000	x	142/142	=	510,000

f. IN THE UNITED STATES

In the U.S. you can obtain current consumer price index (CPI) information by telephoning your local Department of Commerce district office and asking them to give you the desired data from Table 784 of the Statistical Abstract of the United States produced by the U.S. Department of Commerce, Bureau of the Census.

This CPI information can be obtained for the past 10 years for any of 28 major city/metropolitan areas.

If you would like a copy of the entire Statistical Abstract of the United States, which contains much information that might be useful to you in your business, you can obtain it from:

Superintendent of Documents
U.S. Government Printing Office
Washington, D.C. 20402
(202) 783-3238

g. IN CANADA

In Canada, you can obtain current consumer price index (CPI) information by telephoning your local Statistics Canada office and asking them to give you the desired data from Table 7 in Catalogue #62-001 The Consumer Price Index.

This CPI information can be obtained by the month or by annual average for any of 15 major cities in Canada, or for the country in general, for each of the past 5 years.

If you would like a copy of this catalogue, you can get it at any government agency bookstore at a nominal cost.

Alternatively, you can write to:

Publications, Sales and Service
Statistics Canada
Ottawa, Ontario
K1A 0T6

6
BALANCE SHEET ANALYSIS

In the previous chapter we had a look at some of the ways in which income statement information can be presented and analyzed. In this chapter we will have a look at balance sheet analysis, in conjunction with some income statement information.

Harry runs a wholesale goods store and owns both the land and building. He wants to do a balance sheet analysis to see how well he is doing. Using a balance sheet and income statement (Samples #8 and #9), he can calculate a number of important factors.

a. CURRENT RATIO

The current ratio is one of the most commonly used ratios to measure a small business's liquidity or its ability to meet its short-term debts (current liabilities) without difficulty. The equation for this ratio is —

$$\frac{\text{Current assets}}{\text{Current liabilities}}$$

Using the numbers from Harry's balance sheet (Sample #8) the ratio is:

$$\frac{\$132,000}{\$108,000} = 1.22$$

The ratio shows that for every $1.00 of short-term debt (current liabilities) there is $1.22 of current assets. A rule of thumb in business is that there should be $2.00 or more of current assets for each $1.00 of current liabilities.

However, some businesses can frequently operate without difficulty with a current ratio of less than two to one.

Each business must determine what its most effective current ratio is in order to have a current ratio position that neither creates short-term liquidity problems (too low a ratio) nor sacrifices profitability for safety (too high a ratio). If the ratio is too high you have too much money tied up in working capital (current assets less current liabilities) that is not earning a profit.

b. QUICK RATIO

Since there are some not very liquid assets included in the calculation of the current ratio, bankers and other lenders frequently like to calculate the acid test ratio. Only the cash and accounts receivable make up the numerator of this ratio:

$$\frac{\text{Cash + receivables}}{\text{Current liabilities}}$$

Harry's ratio is —

$$\frac{\$85,000 + \$15,000}{\$108,000} = 0.93$$

Lenders, under normal circumstances, like to see this ratio at 1 to 1 or higher. In Harry's case it is 0.93 to 1, or less than what is normally considered an acceptable level.

c. ACCOUNTS RECEIVABLE

Many small businesses run into financial and cash flow difficulties because they lose control over their accounts receivable. There are a couple of useful ratios for assessing the receivables situation. One of these is the calculation of the accounts receivable turnover, and the other is the calculation of the number of days sales tied up in receivables.

1. Accounts receivable turnover

The accounts receivable turnover is calculated as follows:

SAMPLE #8
BALANCE SHEET

HARRY'S WHOLESALE LTD.
Balance Sheet as at December 31, 199-

ASSETS			LIABILITIES & OWNER'S EQUITY		
Current asset:			**Current liabilities:**		
Cash	$ 15,000		Accounts payable	$ 56,000	
Accounts receivable	85,000		Accrued expenses	4,000	
Inventory	27,000		Income tax payable	22,000	
Prepaid expenses	5,000		Current mortgage payable	26,000	
Total current assets		$132,000	Total current liabilities		$108,000
Fixed assets:			**Long-term liability:**		
Land	$ 61,000		Mortgage payable		487,000
Building	882,000		Total liabilities		$595,000
Equipment	246,000				
	$1,189,000		**Owner's equity:**		
Accumulated depreciation	(422,000)	767,000	Common shares	$200,000	
Total fixed assets		$899,000	Retained earnings	104,000	
			Total owner's equity		304,000
					$ 899,000

HARRY'S WHOLESALE LTD.
Income Statement for Year Ending
December 31, 199-

Sales	$956,000
Cost of goods sold	521,000
Gross profit	$435,000
Operating expenses	303,000
Profit before interest	$132,000
Interest expense	52,000
Profit before income tax	$ 80,000
Income tax	40,000
Net profit	$ 40,000

$$\frac{\text{Credit sales for year}}{\text{Accounts receivable}}$$

Harry looked at the sales on his income statement (all sales were made on a credit basis) and the accounts receivable on his balance sheet. His turnover ratio is —

$$\frac{\$956,000}{\$85,000} = 11.25 \text{ times}$$

In a typical business that succeeds in collecting payments of accounts close to a 30-day limit, an annual turnover of 12 would be acceptable. Harry is within that limit. If the turnover was much lower than 12 it would not normally be considered good.

2. Day's sales in receivables

Another way of assessing the receivables situation is to calculate the day's sales outstanding in receivables. This requires two steps. First you must calculate the average daily credit sales:

$$\frac{\text{Credit sales for year}}{260}$$

The figure of 260 is used as the denominator because Harry runs a wholesale business that is open for 5 days a week for 52 weeks in a year. If the business were a retail operation open 6 days a week, the denominator would be 52 x 6 or 312. If the business were open 7 days a week (e.g., a restaurant), then the denominator would be 365.

In Harry's case it is —

$$\frac{\$956,000}{260} = \$3,677 \text{ of credit sales per day}$$

The next step is to calculate the average number of days that the year-end accounts receivable figure (from the balance sheet) represents. The equation for this is —

$$\frac{\text{Accounts receivable at year-end}}{\text{Average daily credit sales}}$$

Harry's calculations are:

$$\frac{\$85,000}{\$3,677} = 23 \text{ days}$$

Note that this figure of 23 days (in Harry's case) is "working" days and would be the equivalent of about a calendar month.

Whenever the accounts receivable results indicate that the turnover rate or number of days outstanding are over the desirable limit of, let us say, 30 calendar days, you need to ask and answer the following typical questions:

44

(a) Can the business carry these overdue accounts without impairing its cash position?

(b) Is a 30-day limit normal for our type of business?

(c) Have we been unwise in extending more than 30 days' credit to some customers?

(d) Can anything be done to encourage more prompt payment of outstanding accounts?

(e) Would an interest charge on overdue accounts speed up collections?

(f) Has the bad debt loss amount increased because some customers do not pay within the normal 30-day limit?

d. INVENTORY TURNOVER

The amount of cash tied up in inventory can, at times, lead to serious consequences. One measure of acceptability of inventory level is the inventory turnover calculation:

$$\frac{\text{Cost of goods sold}}{\text{Average inventory}}$$

Average inventory is normally defined as —

$$\frac{\text{Beginning of the year inventory + end of the year inventory}}{2}$$

Harry's inventory figure from his balance sheet is the average figure. The turnover rate would then be —

$$\frac{\$421,000}{\$27,000} = 19.3 \text{ times for the year}$$

This is a little more than 11½ times a month.

You must try to determine what the normal or standard inventory turnover rate is for your particular type of business and watch for deviations of your turnover from this standard.

e. TOTAL LIABILITIES TO TOTAL EQUITY RATIO

The total assets in a business can be financed by either liabilities (debt) or equity (shares and retained earnings). The total liabilities to total equity ratio (commonly called the debt to equity ratio) illustrates the relationship between these two forms of financing. It is calculated as follows:

$$\frac{\text{Total liabilities}}{\text{Total owners' equity}}$$

Harry's figures are —

$$\frac{\$595,000}{\$304,000} = 1.96$$

This ratio tells Harry that for each $1.00 that he has invested, the creditors, or lenders, have invested $1.96. The higher the creditors' ratio, or debt to equity ratio, the higher the risk to the creditor or lender. In such circumstances, if a business needed additional money to expand its operations, it might find it difficult to borrow the funds.

The contradiction is that while your creditors prefer not to have the debt to equity ratio too high, you will often find it more profitable to have it as high as possible. A high debt to equity ratio is known as having high leverage. Using leverage, or trading on the equity, is discussed later in this chapter.

f. NUMBER OF TIMES INTEREST EARNED

Another measure that creditors sometimes use to measure the safety of their investment is the number of times interest is earned during a year. The equation for this is —

$$\frac{\text{Profit before interest and income tax}}{\text{Interest expense}}$$

46

Harry's figures are —

$$\frac{\$132,000}{\$52,000} = 2.54 \text{ times a year}$$

Generally an investor or creditor considers the investment safe if interest is earned two or more times a year.

g. NET PROFIT TO SALES RATIO

When Harry wanted to measure his profitability, he used the common measure of net profit to sales ratio:

$$\frac{\text{Net profit}}{\text{Sales}} \times 100$$

His figures are —

$$\frac{\$40,000}{\$956,000} \times 100 = 4.2\%$$

Harry saw that out of each $1 of sales there were 4.2¢ net profit. The net profit to sales ratio of many businesses falls in the range of 3% to 7% (however, there are exceptions to this guideline). In absolute terms these percentages may not be too meaningful because they do not necessarily truly represent the profitability of the business.

Consider the following two cases:

	Business A	Business B
Sales	$100,000	$100,000
Net profit	$5,000	$10,000
Net profit to sales ratio	5%	10%

With the same sales it seems that Business B is better. Business B is making twice as much net profit, in absolute terms, as is Business A ($10,000 to $5,000). This doubling of net profit is supported by the net profit to sales ratio (10% to 5%).

47

If these were two similar businesses, or two branches of the same business, these figures would indicate the relative effectiveness of the management of each in controlling costs and generating a satisfactory level of profit. However, to determine the profitability of a small business, you need to relate the net profit to the investment by calculating the return on the owners' equity or return on investment.

h. RETURN ON OWNERS' EQUITY

The equation for return on owners' equity is —

$$\frac{\text{Net profit}}{\text{Owners' equity}} \times 100$$

Harry's figures are —

$$\frac{\$40,000}{\$304,000} \times 100 = 13.2\%$$

This ratio shows the effectiveness of Harry's use of his own funds (or equity).

How high should the ratio be? This is a matter of personal opinion. If an investor could put money either into the bank at 10% interest rate or into a business investment at only 8% with more risk involved, the bank might look like the better of the two choices. Many people feel that 15% (after tax) is a reasonable return for the owner of a small business (with all its risks) to expect.

Now we can return to the Business A and Business B situation discussed earlier. Assume that the investment in A was $40,000 and in B $80,000. The return on the investment would be —

BUSINESS A

$$\frac{\$5,000}{\$40,000} \times 100 = 12.5\%$$

BUSINESS B

$$\frac{\$10,000}{\$80,000} \times 100 = 12.5\%$$

Despite the wide difference in net profit and in net profit to sales ratio (calculated earlier), there is no difference between the two businesses as far as profitability is concerned. They are both equally as good, each yielding a 12.5% return on the investment, or return on owners' equity.

i. RETURN ON ASSETS

Lenders also sometimes like to calculate the return on assets. The equation for this is —

$$\frac{\text{Profit before interest and income tax}}{\text{Total assets}} \times 100$$

In Harry's case the result is —

$$\frac{\$132,000}{\$899,000} = \times 100 \ 14.7\%$$

This result can then be compared with current interest rates on borrowed money. For example, a lender from whom Harry wanted to borrow money to expand his business might have a 15% current interest rate. If the expanded premises resulted in additional profits before interest and income tax of only 14.7%, the lender might question whether Harry's business can even meet the additional interest payments.

j. NET PROFIT TO ASSETS

As an alternative to borrowing money for expansion, Harry could lend money to the business. The net profit to assets ratio will give him some idea of the return he could expect. The equation is —

$$\frac{\text{Net profit}}{\text{Total assets}}$$

Harry's present profit to assets figures are —

$$\frac{\$40,000}{\$899,000} = 0.044 \text{ or } 4.4\%$$

If that were the return on any additional investment, Harry might be better off to leave his money in the bank.

k. FINANCIAL LEVERAGE

Alice and Sue are business partners. They are considering leasing a new building for their business. They need $250,000 for equipment and working capital. They have the cash, so they could use all their own money for 100% equity financing, or they could use 50% of their own money and borrow 50% (debt financing) at a 10% interest rate.

Regardless of which financing method they use, sales and all operating costs will be the same. With either choice, they will have $50,000 profit before interest and taxes.

There is no interest expense with 100% equity financing. Interest will have to be paid with debt financing. However, interest expense is tax deductible.

Assuming a tax rate of 50% on taxable profit, Sample #10 shows the comparative operating results and the "return on investment" (ROI) for each of the two options.

In this situation, not only do Alice and Sue make a better ROI under a 50/50 debt/equity ratio (15% ROI versus 10%), but they still have $125,000 cash that they can invest in a second venture.

Because a 50/50 debt to equity ratio proved to be more profitable than 100% equity financing, Alice and Sue wondered if an 80/20 debt to equity ratio would be even more profitable.

In other words, what would the ROI be if they used only $50,000 of their own money and borrowed the remaining $200,000 at 10%? Sample #11 shows the result of this more highly levered situation.

Under this third option, the return on initial investment has now increased to 30%, and Alice and Sue still have

$200,000 cash, enough for four more similar business ventures.

1. Advantages of leverage

The advantages of leverage are obvious: the higher the debt to equity ratio, the higher the ROI will be. However, this holds true only if profit (before interest) as a percent of debt is greater than the interest rate to be paid on the debt. For example, if the debt interest rate is 10%, the profit before interest must be more than 10% of the money borrowed (the debt) for leverage to be profitable.

2. Risks of leverage

With high debt (high leverage) there is a risk. If profit declines, the more highly levered the business is, the sooner it will be in financial difficulty.

In the 50/50 financing in Sample #10 (relatively low leverage), profit before interest and income tax could decline from $50,000 to $12,500 before net profit would be zero. In Sample #11 (relatively high leverage), profit before interest and income tax could decline from $50,000 to only $20,000.

What is the "best" debt to equity ratio for a business? There is no best ratio. The figure differs from one type of business to another, and even between two similar types of business, since there are so many variables to be considered at any particular time. These variables include the relative profitability of the business, current interest rates, alternative uses for your equity money, the present economic climate, and many others.

However, in general, lenders like to see a debt/equity ratio that is on a par with published debt/equity ratio figures for similar businesses or industries.

SAMPLE #10
EFFECT OF LEVERAGE ON ROI

	100% equity	50% equity 50% debt
Total investment required	$250,000	$250,000
Debt financing at 10%		$125,000
Equity financing	$250,000	125,000
Profit before interest and tax	$50,000	$50,000
Interest expense 10% of $125,00		(12,500)
Profit before tax	$50,000	$37,500
Income tax 50%	(25,000)	(18,750)
Net profit	$25,000	$18,750
Return on partners' investment	$\dfrac{\$25,000}{\$250,000} \times 100$ = 10%	$\dfrac{\$18,750}{\$125,000} \times 100$ = 15%

SAMPLE #11
EFFECT OF HIGH LEVERAGE ON ROI

Total investment required	$250,000
Debt financing at 10% Equity financing	$200,000 50,000
Profit before interest and tax Interest 10% of $200,000	$ 50,000 (20,000)
Profit before tax Income tax 50%	$ 30,000 (15,000)
Net profit Return on partners' investment	$ 15,000 $\frac{\$15,000}{\$50,000} \times 200 = 30\%$

7
INTERNAL CONTROL

In a very small business, few internal controls are required since the owner/operator generally handles all the cash coming in and going out and, by being present, ensures the smooth and efficient operation of the business.

In larger businesses, one person control is not feasible. In fact, in larger businesses, it is necessary to organize operations into various departments and to draw up a plan of the organization, or an organization chart. Indeed, the organization chart becomes the foundation of a good internal control system since it establishes lines of communication and levels of authority and responsibility.

a. SYSTEM REQUIREMENTS

A good system of internal control requires the following:

(a) Methods and procedures for the employees in the various jobs to follow to ensure they act according to your policies, achieve operational efficiency, and protect assets (such as cash and inventory) from waste, theft, or fraud

(b) Reliable forms and reports that measure the efficiency and effectiveness of the business and provide information (usually of an accounting and financial nature) that, when analyzed, will identify problem areas

This information must be accurate and timely if it is to be useful. it must also be cost effective; in other words, the benefits (cost savings) of an internal control system must be greater than the cost of its implementation and continuation.

Information produced must also be useful. If the information is not used, then you have wasted effort and money. In the two preceding chapters you saw how some of the information provided by the internal control/accounting system can be used to monitor the progress of the business.

b. PRINCIPLES OF INTERNAL CONTROL

1. Management attitude and supervision

Most employees are honest by nature but, because of a poor internal control system or, worse still, complete absence of controls, are sometimes tempted into dishonesty. If you don't care, why should your employees?

Control systems, by themselves, solve no problems. They do not absolutely protect your business against fraud or theft. A system of control may point out what is happening, but it is important to remember that even with a good control system, collusion (two or more employees working together for dishonest purposes) may go undetected for a long time. For this and other reasons any control system that you implement must be supervised by you or your delegate.

2. Establish responsibilities

One of the prerequisites for good internal control is a clear definition of job responsibilities. This goes beyond designing an organization chart. For example, in the case of deliveries of products or supplies to the business, who will do the receiving? Will it be a clerk/receiver, the maintenance employee, or you? And once that is determined, how is receiving to be handled?

3. Written procedures

Once responsibilities have been determined, and procedures established, these procedures should be put into writing. In this way employees responsible will know what the procedures are. Written procedures are particularly important where turnover of employees is relatively high and continuous employee training to support the internal control system is required.

4. Forms and reports

Once procedures have been established and the employees given detailed written guidelines about how to perform tasks, you need to establish standards of performance. This requires designing forms and reports to provide information about all the business's operations. Properly designed forms and reports provide you with the information you need to determine if standards are being met and to make decisions that will improve the standards, increase productivity, and ultimately produce higher profits.

5. System monitoring and review

Any system of control must be monitored to ensure that it is continuing to provide the desired information. The system must therefore be flexible enough to be changed to suit different needs. If a reporting form needs to be changed, then it should be changed.

If a form becomes redundant, than it should be scrapped or be replaced by one that is more suitable. To have employees complete forms and/or reports that no one looks at is costly, and employees quickly become disillusioned when there seems to be no purpose to what they are asked to do.

One of your major responsibilities in internal control is constant review of the system. This review is necessary because the system will become obsolete as conditions change. In small businesses the review of the internal control system is the responsibility of the owner/operator. In larger businesses, particularly those with accounting or bookkeeping employees, the review responsibility is turned over to the employees in that department.

6. Rotate jobs

Finally, wherever possible, jobs should be rotated. Obviously this cannot be easily done in a small business with few employees. In a larger business employees may appreciate being moved from one job to another from time to time.

Job rotation has a number of advantages. Employees who know they are not going to be doing the same job for any length of time are less likely to be dishonest since the possibilities or collusion are reduced. Job rotation keeps employees from becoming bored from constantly carrying out the same tasks. It also builds flexibility into job assignments and gives employees a better understanding of how the various jobs relate to each other.

c. CASH RECEIPTS

Good cash handling and internal control procedures are not only important to the business owner or manager, but also to the employees involved, since a good system will show that employees have handled their responsibilities correctly and honestly.

All cash receipts should be deposited intact each day in the bank. A deposit slip stamped by the bank should be kept by the business. This is a form of receipt. If all cash received each day is deposited daily, no one who handles it will be tempted to "borrow" cash for a few days for personal use. It also ensures that no payments are made in cash on invoices. If this were allowed, a dishonest employee could make out a false invoice and collect cash for it.

Employees who handle cash (and other assets such as inventories) should be bonded. In this way losses are less likely to occur since the employees know they will have to answer to the insurance company if shortages arise.

1. Separate recordkeeping and asset control

One of the most important principles of good cash control is to separate recording information about cash from the actual control of cash.

Consider the accounts of the people or companies to whom you sell goods or services on credit. These accounts are an asset. Checks received in payment are given to the cashier who then records the payments on the accounts.

These checks, along with other cash and checks received from customers, are turned in as part of the total remittance at the end of the cashier's shift. There is nothing wrong with this procedure as long as the cashier is honest.

2. Lapping

A dishonest cashier could practice a procedure known as lapping.

So-so Sales Inc. owes you $150 on account. When it receives its statement at the month-end, it sends in a check for $150. Leta Liar, your cashier, does not record the payment on the account of So-so Sales Inc. Instead, she simply puts the check in the cash drawer and removes $150 in bills for personal use. Her remittance at the end of the shift will balance, but So-so Sales' account will still show an unpaid amount of $150.

When Better Sales Company, which has an account for $170, sends in its payments, Leta Liar records $150 as a payment on So-so Sales' account, puts the $170 check in the cash drawer and removes a further $20 in cash for personal use.

A few days later Best Buy Company makes a payment of $200 on its account. The cashier records $170 on Better Sales account, puts the $200 check in the cash drawer and takes out $30 more in cash.

This lapping of accounts will eventually increase to the point where Leta Liar can no longer cover a particular account and the fraud will be discovered. However, the outstanding account may be so large that the misappropriated cash cannot be recovered from the dishonest cashier.

To help prevent this type of loss, cash receiving and recording on accounts should be separate functions. Checks or cash received in the mail in payment of accounts should be deposited directly in the bank by you or a responsible employee. The employee looking after the accounts is simply given a list of account names and amounts received, and the appropriate accounts can be credited without that person handling any money. In other words, the responsibility for handling cash and recording payments on accounts is separated.

d. CASH DISBURSEMENTS

For minor disbursements that have to be handled by cash, a petty cash fund should be established. You should put enough cash into this fund to take care of about one month's transactions. The fund should be the responsibility of one person only. Payments out of it must be supported by a receipt, voucher, or memorandum explaining the purpose of the disbursement.

When the cash fund is almost used up, the supporting receipts, vouchers, and memoranda can be turned in, and the head cashier or manager can replenish the fund with cash up to the original amount. Receipts, vouchers, or memoranda turned in should be stamped "paid," or canceled in some similar way, so that they cannot be reused.

All other disbursements should be made by check and supported by an approved invoice. All checks should be numbered in sequence. Checks should be prepared by you or another responsible person, but that other person should have no authority to sign the checks.

As checks are prepared, the related invoices should be canceled in some way so that there is no possibility of fraud. Any checks spoiled in preparation should be voided so that they cannot be reused.

1. Bank reconciliation

One control that is necessary in a good internal system is a monthly bank reconciliation. At each month-end you should obtain a statement from your bank showing each daily deposit, the amount of each check paid, and other items added to or subtracted from the bank balance. The canceled (paid) checks should accompany this statement.

To ensure control, the bank reconciliation should not be carried out by the person who records cash receipts or disbursements, otherwise "kiting" could occur.

Kiting occurs when a check is written or drawn on one bank account without recording it as a disbursement. The check is then deposited in a second bank account and the deposit is recorded. As a result the cash amount in the first bank is overstated (and cash can be removed) by an amount equal to the unrecorded check.

The steps in the reconciliation are as follows:

(a) Compare and mark off on the statement the amount of each check received back with your bank statement.

(b) Arrange your canceled (paid) checks in number sequence.

(c) Verify the amount of each canceled check with the amount of your check register or journal. Make a note of any outstanding checks. An outstanding check is one made out by you but not yet paid by the bank.

(d) To the bank statement balance add deposits made by you and not yet recorded by the bank and subtract any outstanding checks.

(e) Add any amounts to your bank balance figure added by the bank on its statement but not yet recorded by you (e.g., bank interest earned on deposits) and subtract any deductions made by the bank (such as automatic payments on loans and interest or service charges).

Once these steps have been completed, the two balances should agree. If they do not, the work should be rechecked. If the figures still do not agree, errors have been made, either by the bank or on your books. These errors should be discovered and corrected.

To see how a reconciliation is carried out consider the following figures:

Bank statement balance	$4,456
Company bank balance	6,848
Deposit in transit	2,896
Outstanding checks — #355	372
#372	40
Interest earned on deposits	98
Bank service charge	6

The reconciliation would be as follows:

BANK BALANCE	YOUR BALANCE
$4,456	$6,848
2,896	98
(372)	(6)
(40)	
_____	_____
$6,940	$6,940

8
COST MANAGEMENT

Most of the cash from sales in a business goes toward expenses — as much as 90¢ or more of each sales dollar may be used to pay for expenses. Therefore, expense or cost management is important.

a. COMMON BUSINESS COSTS

In order to manage costs you must understand that there are many types of cost. If you can recognize the type of cost you are dealing with, you can make better decisions about it.

1. Discretionary costs

A discretionary cost is one that may, or may not, be incurred at the discretion of a particular person — usually the business owner or manager. Non-emergency maintenance is an example. The building exterior could be painted this year, or the painting could be postponed until next year. In either case sales should not be affected. As the owner/manager you have the choice. You can use your own discretion.

2. Relevant costs

A relevant cost is one that makes a difference to a decision. For example, Rose's Retail Store is considering replacing one cash register with another. The relevant costs would be the cost of the new machine (less any trade-in on the old one), the cost of training employees on the new equipment, and any change in maintenance and stationery supply costs on the new machine.

3. Sunk costs

A sunk cost is a cost already incurred and about which nothing can be done. It cannot affect any future decisions. For example, if Rose's Retail Store had spent $250 for its accountant to study the relative merits of different cash registers available, that $250 is a sunk cost. It cannot make any difference to the decision.

4. Fixed costs

Fixed costs are those that, over the short run (a year or less), do not change or vary with volume. Examples of these would be the salary of the business's manager, fire insurance expenses, and interest on a mortgage. Over the long run all these costs can change. But, in the short run, they would normally be fixed.

5. Variable costs

A variable cost is one that varies on a linear basis with sales. Very few costs are strictly linear, but some are. For example, rent based on sales, or the remuneration of employees who are paid solely on a commission basis, are variable costs.

6. Semifixed or semivariable costs

Most costs do not fit neatly into the fixed or variable category. Most have an element of fixed expense and an element of variable, and the variable element is not always variable directly to sales. For example, the cost of goods sold (since higher sales often result in item price cuts), labor, maintenance, and energy costs would all fall into this category.

In order to make useful decisions it is advantageous to break down these semifixed or semivariable costs into their two elements. (See chapter 9.)

7. Standard costs

A standard cost is what the cost should be for a given volume or level of sales. An example would be a $2 widget that National Widget Co. produces. If 100 are sold, the standard cost would be $200. If 500 were sold, the standard cost should be $1,000.

b. COST ANALYSIS — WHICH PIECE OF EQUIPMENT TO BUY?

A good analysis of the type of cost you are dealing with will help in decision making in your business.

One of the problems that all managers face is that of choosing between alternatives such as what selling prices to charge, which employees to hire, and how to spend the advertising budget. One area of such decision making where a knowledge of costs is helpful is that of selecting a piece of equipment.

You have asked your accountant to research the postage machine equipment available and to recommend the two best pieces of equipment on the market. A decision will then be made by you about which of the two to use. The accountant's fee for this work is $500. This $500 is a sunk cost. It has to be paid regardless of your decision and, indeed, would have to be paid even if you decided not to purchase either piece of equipment.

The accountant reported the following information:

	BEST BUY POSTAGE MACHINE	BETTER YET POSTAGE MACHINE
Initial cost	$10,000	$8,000
Economic life	10 years	10 years
Trade in value	0	0
Annual depreciation	$1,000	$800
Initial training	600	1,100
Annual maintenance	300	200
Annual cost of forms	700	800
Annual wage cost	32,000	32,000

The relevant costs from this information are —

	BEST BUY POSTAGE MACHINE	BETTER YET POSTAGE MACHINE
Annual depreciation	$1,000	$ 800
Initial training	600	1,100
Annual maintenance	300	200
Annual cost of forms	700	800
Total year 1 cost	$2,600	$2,900

This information shows that in year 1 Best Buy is cheaper than Better Yet by $300. However, this saving is in year 1 only. You need to look ahead to see what the relevant costs are over the full economic life of the equipment.

After the first year, the initial training cost would be eliminated (i.e., it is now a sunk cost). The total cost for years 2 to 10 (nine times the annual cost) would be $18,000 for Best Buy and $16,200 for Better Yet.

To complete the calculation, add the total cost for years 2 to 10 to the cost for year 1. The total 10-year cost for Best Buy is $20,600 and for Better Yet $19,100. Despite year 1, the total 10-year cost is $1,500 less with the Better Yet postage machine.

In the final decision, out-of-pocket costs may not be the only factor to consider. A more comprehensive look at this type of investment decision is in chapter 13.

c. SHOULD YOU CLOSE IN THE OFF SEASON?

One of the uses of a break down of fixed and variable costs is to decide whether or not to close in the off season.

Mike's resort motel has the following annual income statement:

Sales	$150,000
Expenses	130,000
Net profit	$20,000

Mike decided to do an analysis of his sales and costs by the month. He found that for ten months he was making money and for two months he had a loss. (See Sample #12.)

Mike's analysis seems to indicate that he should close to eliminate the $10,000 loss during the two-month loss period. But, if he does, the fixed costs for the two months ($24,000) will have to be paid out of the ten months' profits, and $30,000 (ten months' net profit) less the two months' fixed costs of $24,000 will reduce his annual net profit to $6,000 from its present $20,000. If he does not want a reduction in annual net profit, he should not close.

There might be other factors, in such a situation, that need to be considered and that would reinforce the decision to stay open. For example, there could be sizable additional close down and start up costs that would have to be included in the calculation of the cost of closing.

Also, Mike needs to consider the following:

(a) Would key employees return after an extended vacation?

(b) Is there a large enough pool of skilled labor available and willing to work on a seasonal basis only?

(c) Would there be recurring training time (and costs) at the start of each new season?

These are some of the kinds of questions that would have to be answered before any final decision to close was made.

d. WHICH BUSINESS TO BUY

Business owners/managers have to make choices between alternatives on a day-to-day basis, but they also must decide, on a larger scale, about going into business, expanding an existing business, or buying a new business. The following situation involves fixed and variable costs.

Martha Makabuk has an opportunity to take over one of two similar existing businesses. The two businesses are close to each other in location, have the same type of clientele and size of operation, and the asking price is the same for each.

Each is doing $1,000,000 a year in sales, and each has a net profit of $100,000 a year. With only this information it is difficult for Martha to decide which would be the more profitable investment. She did a cost analysis to find some of the differences. (See Sample #13.)

1. Structure of costs

Although the sales and net profit are the same for each business, the structure of their costs is different, and this will affect the decision about which one could be more profitable.

Martha Makabuk is optimistic about the future. She feels that, without any change in fixed costs, she can increase annual sales in either business by 10%.

But the net profit for each of the two businesses will not increase by the same amount. Big Business' variable costs are 50%. This means that, out of each dollar of additional sales, it will have variable expenses of 50¢ and a net profit of 50¢ (since fixed costs do not change.)

Assuming that a 10% increase in sales would be achieved and no new fixed costs would be added, Martha recalculated the income statements of the two businesses. (See Sample #14.)

Note that Big Business' net profit has gone up by $50,000 to $150,000, but Broad Business' has gone up by $70,000 to $170,000. In this situation Broad Business Co. would be the better investment.

e. HIGH OPERATING LEVERAGE

In chapter 6 we discussed the concept of high financial leverage (high debt to equity) for a business. By the same logic, a business that has high fixed costs relative to variable costs is said to have high operating leverage. From a profit point of view it will do better in times or rising sales than a business with low operating leverage (low fixed costs relative to variable costs).

A business with low fixed costs, however, will be better off when sales start to decline.

Suppose two businesses are going to have a decline in sales of 10% from the present $1,000,000 level and that there will be no change in fixed costs. Sample #15 shows that, with declining sales, Business A's net profit will be higher than Business B's.

In fact, if sales decline far enough, Business B will be in financial difficulty long before Business A. If the break-even point were calculated (the break-even point is that level of sales at which there will be neither a profit nor a loss), Business As sales could go down to $800,000 while Business B would be in difficulty at $857,000. This is illustrated in Sample #16.

You could determine the break-even level of sales by trial and error (although this would be rather tedious), but there is a formula available for quick calculation of this level. The formula and a more indepth discussion of fixed and variable costs and how this can be of great value in making many types of decisions is covered in chapter 10.

SAMPLE #12
SALES AND COSTS ANALYSIS

Mike's Motel Sales and Costs by Season			
	10 months	2 months	Annual total
Sales	$135,000	$15,000	$150,000
Variable costs	$25,000	$1,000	$26,000
Fixed costs	$80,000	$24,000	$104,000
Total costs	$105,000	$25,000	$130,000
Net profit (loss)	$30,000	($10,000)	$20,000

SAMPLE #13
COST ANALYSIS

	Big Business Co.		Broad Business Co.	
	Dollars	Percent	Dollars	Percent
Sales	$1,000,000	100%	$1,000,000	100.0%
Variable costs	500,000	50%	300,000	30.0%
Fixed costs	400,000	40%	600,000	60.0%
Total costs	$900,000	90%	$900,000	90.0%
Net profit	$100,000	10%	$100,000	10.0%

SAMPLE #14
COST ANALYSIS WITH INCREASED SALES

	Big Business Co.		Broad Business Co.	
	Dollars	Percent	Dollars	Percent
Sales	$1,100,000	100.0%	$1,100,000	100.0%
Variable costs	550,000	50.0%	330,000	30.0%
Fixed costs	400,000	36.4%	600,000	54.5%
Total costs	$950,000	86.4%	$930,000	84.5%
Net profit	$150,000	13.6%	$170,000	15.5%

SAMPLE #15
COST ANALYSIS WITH DECREASED SALES

	Big Business Co.		Broad Business Co.	
	Dollars	Percent	Dollars	Percent
Sales	$900,000	100.0%	$900,000	100.0%
Variable costs	450,000	50.0%	270,000	30.0%
Fixed costs	400,000	44.4%	600,000	66.7%
Total costs	$850,000	94.4%	$870,000	96.7%
Net profit	$50,000	5.6%	$30,000	3.3%

SAMPLE #16
COST ANALYSIS WITH BREAK-EVEN SALES

	Business A		Business B	
	Dollars	Percent	Dollars	Percent
Sales	$ 800,000	100.0%	$857,000	100.0%
Variable costs	400,000	50.0%	257,000	30.0%
Fixed costs	400,000	50.0%	600,000	70.0%
Total costs	$ 800,000	100.0%	$ 857,000	100.0%
Net profit	0	0	0	0.0

9

FIXED AND VARIABLE COSTS

Once costs have been broken down into their fixed and variable elements, valuable information is then available for use in decision making. Although some costs can be quickly identified as either fixed or variable, the majority fall into the semifixed or semivariable category. These will be referred to as "semi costs" from now on.

A number of different methods are available for breaking down these semi costs into fixed and variable. The two illustrated here are maximum/minimum methods and multipoint graph method.

a. MAXIMUM/MINIMUM METHOD

Ralph owns a repair service company dealing with retail customers. It has annual labor costs of $120,000. Since the cost of labor is closely related to the number of customers the business handles, Ralph needs a month-by-month breakdown of the sales and the related wage costs for each month. (This information could be broken down by week, but there should be sufficient accuracy for all practical purposes with a monthly analysis). The monthly breakdown of sales and wage costs is given in Sample #17.

Note that the month of January has the word "minimum" alongside it. In January, sales and wage costs were at their lowest for the year. In contrast, in August costs were at their "maximum."

SAMPLE #17
MAXIMUM/MINIMUM
ANALYSIS OF SALES AND WAGES

	Sales	Wages
January (minimum)	$ 5,000	$ 7,200
February	9,000	8,000
March	14,000	9,000
April	13,000	10,700
May	13,000	12,300
June	15,000	12,000
July	21,000	13,000
August	21,000	13,200
September	15,000	11,900
October	10,000	7,600
November	10,000	7,600
December	7,000	7,500
Totals	$153,000	$120,000

There are three steps in the maximum/minimum method:

(a) Deduct the minimum from the maximum figures:

	Sales	Wages
August (maximum)	$21,000	$13,200
January (minimum)	5,000	7,200
Differences	$16,000	$6,000

(b) Divide the wage difference by the sales difference:

$$\frac{\$6,000}{\$16,000} = \$0.375 = \text{variable costs per \$1 of sales}$$

(c) Use the variable costs per $1 of sales from step (b) to calculate the total fixed costs per month:

August total wages	$13,200
variable costs:	
$21,000 x $0.375	7,875
Fixed wage costs	$ 5,325

73

Ralph could equally well have used January (the minimum month) in step (c) with no change in the result. The calculated fixed costs are $5,325 a month of $63,900 a year (12 x $5,325). Ralph rounded this figure to the nearest thousand ($64,000) for further calculations.

Now Ralph can break down his total annual wage costs into fixed and variable elements:

Total annual wages	$120,000
Fixed costs	64,000
Variable costs	$ 56,000

The calculation of the monthly fixed costs has been illustrated by arithmetical means. The maximum/minimum figures could equally well have been plotted on a graph, as illustrated in Sample #18.

SAMPLE #18
MAXIMUM/MINIMUM GRAPH

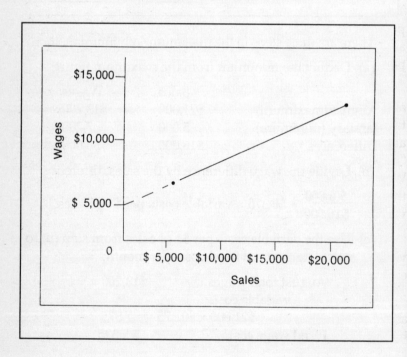

74

Ralph first plots the maximum figure as the upper right-hand point, and the minimum figure as the lower left-hand point. The two points are then joined by a solid line, which is continued by a dotted line. The fixed costs figure is where the dotted line intersects the vertical axis.

Ralph has accurately drawn the graph, so the same monthly fixed wage costs figure of approximately $5,300 is arrived at.

The maximum/minimum method is quick and simple. It uses only two sets of figures. Unfortunately, the sets of figures may not be typical of the relationship between sales and costs for the year (e.g., a one-time wage bonus may have been paid during one of the months selected), thus distorting figures. These distortions can be eliminated, as long as you are aware of them, by adjusting the raw figures.

b. MULTIPOINT GRAPH

To improve on the maximum/minimum method and remove possible distortions in individual month figure, plot the cost and sales figures for each of the 12 months (or however many periods there are involved) on a multipoint graph.

Sample #19 illustrates a multipoint graph for Ralph's sales and wage costs for each of the 12 months. Sales and costs were taken from Sample #17. The graph illustrated is for two variables (sales and wages). In this case wages are given the name "dependent variable" and are plotted on the vertical axis. Wages are dependent on sales — they vary with sales. Sales, therefore, are the independent variable. The independent variable is plotted on the horizontal axis.

Note that in drawing such a graph the point where the vertical and horizontal axes meet is zero. The figures along each axis should then be plotted to scale from zero.

After plotting each of the 12 points, you have what is known as a scatter graph or a series of points scattered around a line that has been drawn through them. A straight line must be drawn.

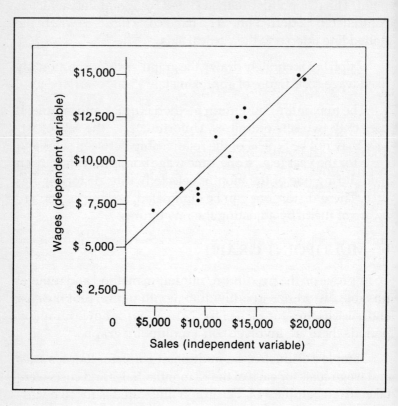

There is no limit to how many straight lines could be drawn through the points. The line you want is the one that, to your eye, seems to fit best. Each person doing this exercise would probably view the line in a slightly different position, but most people with a reasonably good eye would come up with a line that, for all practical purposes, is close enough.

The line should be drawn so that it is continued to the left until it intersects the vertical axis (the dependent variable). The intersect point reading is the fixed costs figure (wages in this case). It is $5,000 (approximately). This is the monthly figure. Converted to annual costs it is $5,000 x 12 = $60,000.

The total annual wage cost would then be broken down as follows:

Total wages	$120,000
Less fixed	60,000
Variable	$60,000

c. DIFFERENCE IN METHODS

With the maximum/minimum method the total annual fixed costs are $64,000. With the multipoint graph method they are $60,000; a difference of $4,000. This difference is primarily because there is a higher risk of inaccuracy with the maximum/minimum method since only two of the twelve months (in Ralph's case) were used and, as was mentioned earlier, these two months may not be typical of the entire year. For this reason the multipoint graph method tends to be more accurate.

Once a method has been selected it should be applied to all the other semi costs so that they too can be broken down into their elements.

10
COST-VOLUME-PROFIT ANALYSIS

Many questions about profit can be asked by the owner of a small business. For example:

- At what level of sales will I start losing money (i.e., what is my break-even sales level)?

- What will my net profit be at a certain level of sales?

- What is the extra sales revenue I need to cover the cost of additional advertising and still give me the profit I want?

- By how much must sales be increased to cover the cost of a wage increase and still give the profit to sales ratio I want?

These and similar questions cannot be answered simply from the traditional income statement. However, the cost-volume-profit (CVP) approach breaks down the income statement into variable and fixed costs and then uses this information for rational decision making. Before you use this method, you must clearly understand the assumptions and limitations of CVP analysis. CVP assumes that —

(a) the costs associated with the present level of sales can be fairly accurately broken down into their fixed and variable elements (see chapter 9),

(b) fixed costs will remain fixed during the period affected by the decision being made, and

(c) variable costs vary directly with sales during the period affected by the decision being made.

CVP analysis is limited to situations where economic and other conditions are assumed to be relatively stable. In highly inflationary times, for example, when it is difficult to predict sales and/or costs more than a few weeks ahead, it would be risky to use CVP for decisions too far into the future. CVP analysis is only a guide to decision making.

The CVP approach might indicate a certain decision, but other factors (such as employee or customer relations) may dictate a decision that contradicts the CVP analysis.

a. CONTRIBUTION MARGIN

Suppose you have the following annual income statement information:

INCOME STATEMENT

Sales		$306,000
Variable costs	$113,000	
Fixed costs	181,000	294,000
Profit		$ 12,000

In CVP analysis, the income statement is sometimes presented in the form of a contribution statement:

CONTRIBUTION STATEMENT

Sales	$306,000
Variable costs	113,000
Contribution to fixed costs	$193,000
Fixed costs	181,000
Profit	$ 12,000

The contribution to the fixed cost figure (in your case $193,000) is commonly referred to as the contribution margin and is simply sales less variable expenses. The profit figure does not change by presenting the fixed and variable costs in this way.

From the above information we can calculate the variable cost as a percent of sales:

$$\frac{\$113,000}{\$306,000} \times 100 = 37\%$$

Therefore, the contribution margin percent is 100% - 37% = 63% or 0.63.

Alternatively, it can be calculated directly by dividing it by the sales:

$$\frac{\$193,000}{\$306,000} \times 100 = 63\% \text{ or } 0.63$$

b. THE CVP EQUATION

The easiest way to use CVP analysis is to use the basic CVP equation:

$$\text{Sales level} = \frac{\text{Fixed costs + profit desired}}{\text{Contribution margin}}$$

c. ANSWERING QUESTIONS

This equation leads to the following questions, and gives the subsequent answers.

Q: At what level of sales will the business break even?
A: The level of sales at which the business will make neither a profit nor a loss (i.e., the break-even point) is —

$$\text{Sales level} = \frac{\$181,000}{.63} + 0 = \$287,302 \text{ rounded to } \$287,000$$

It makes sense to round end figures when using the equation since the breakdown of fixed and variable costs may not be completely accurate in the first place. In most cases, answer to the closest $1,000 would normally be quite acceptable.

Q: At what level of sales will I make $39,000 profit?

A: You can use the above equation for the answer, substituting $39,000 for the profit desired:

$$\text{Sales level} = \frac{\$181,000 + \$39,000}{0.63}$$

$$= \frac{\$220,000}{0.63}$$

$$= 350,000 \ (349,206 \text{ rounded})$$

Q: How much money must my sales increase to cover new fixed costs?

A: Normally, if fixed costs increase and no change is made in selling prices, you would expect profits to decline by the amount of the additional fixed costs. You could then ask how much must sales be increased to compensate for an increase in fixed costs without reducing profit. A simple answer would be that sales have to go up by the same amount as the fixed costs increase. But this is not correct, because to increase sales (with no increase in selling prices) you have to sell more products or service more customers. If you sell more products, your variable costs (such as wages and supplies) are going to increase.

You could arrive at a solution by trial and error, but the CVP equation used so far will solve this kind of question neatly and quickly. Simply add the old fixed costs to the new fixed costs, add the profit desired to the numerator of the equation, and divide as before by the contribution margin.

For example, suppose you wish to spend $5,000 more on advertising a year. To calculate how much more in sales you must have (assuming no price changes) to maintain your present profit level of $12,000, you would use the following figures:

$$\text{Sales level} = \frac{\$181,000 + \$5,000 + \$12,000}{0.63} =$$

$$\frac{\$198,000}{0.63} =$$

$$\$314,286, \text{ rounded to } \$314,000$$

You can easily prove the accuracy of the result (as you can with any solution to a problem using the CVP equation) as follows:

Sales		$314,000
Variable costs —		
37% x $314,000 =	$116,000	
Fixed costs	186,000	
Total costs		302,000
Profit		$ 12,000

The solution to the question tells us sales must be at the $314,000 level — an increase of $8,000 over the present sales level of $306,000.

Q: What additional sales do I need to cover a change in variable costs?
A: A change in the variable costs will change your contribution margin. Therefore the contribution margin must be recalculated, by first recalculating the variable costs percent. Remember that your present variable costs figure of 37% was calculated by dividing total variable costs by total sales and multiplying by 100. Assume an increase in wages is to be put into effect that will increase the variable costs as a percentage of sales from 37% to 39%. The new contribution margin percent will be 100% - 39% = 61% or 0.61. From now on, 0.61 is the denominator in the equation.

Q: What about multiple changes in the variables?
A: So far, you have considered making only one change at a

time. Multiple changes can be handled in the same way without difficulty. For example, assume that $5,000 is to be spent on advertising, that the employees will be given the wage increase (changing the contribution margin to 0.61), and that the profit is to be increased from $12,000 to $20,000. In this case:

$$\text{Sales level} = \frac{\$181,000 + \$5,000 = \$20,000}{0.61}$$

$$= \frac{\$206,000}{0.61} = \$338,000 \text{ rounded or } 337,705$$

To prove this:

Sales		$338,000
Variable costs —		
39% x $338,000 =	$132,000	
Fixed costs	186,000	
Total costs		318,000
Profit		$ 20,000

Q: What about a new investment?
A: The CVP equation has been used in this chapter to illustrate how historical information from accounting records can be used to make decisions about the future. But CVP analysis is equally useful when there is no past accounting information to help you. For example, in a proposed new business, or expansion of an existing one, you simply make intelligent estimates of what the fixed and variable costs are likely to be and then project potential profits from those figures.

d. PERCENT OF CAPACITY

One valuable use of CVP analysis is calculating the percentage of capacity at which a manufacturing firm is operating.

Mel's Manufacturing Company can produce 50 units of its products a day. Mel simply has to multiply the working days times 50 units to establish what production will be if full production is maintained during a specific period (e.g., a week or a month). By comparing actual production with this capacity, a percentage of capacity can be determined.

Mel's company operates 5 days a week, times 52 weeks, or 260 days a year. As 50 units per day is its capacity, the maximum production at 100% capacity would be 13,000 units per year (50 units x 260 days). If actual production is 12,000 units, the percentage of capacity for the year would be —

$$\frac{12,000}{13,000} \times 100 = 92\%$$

You can use the basic CVP equation to answer questions relating to capacity levels. The only difference is that the contribution margin is expressed in dollars, rather than as a percentage. You will remember that contribution margin is sales less variable costs, converted to a percentage of sales. To use contribution margin in dollars, you simply need to find the average sale price of the product and deduct from it the average variable cost.

Mel's total sales for the 12,000 units produced were $120,000. The average sale price is then —

$$\frac{\$120,000}{12,000} = \$10$$

If the total variable costs at this level of sales were $22,000, the average variable costs are —

$$\frac{\$22,200}{12,000} = \$1.85$$

The contribution margin is then $10 less $1.85, or $8.15.

84

If the fixed costs of Mel's manufacturing plan were $90,000, he would then use the CVP equation to solve production questions such as the break-even capacity level:

$$\frac{\$90,000}{\$8.15} = 11,043 \text{ units}$$

This would be:

$$\frac{11,043}{13,000} \times 100 = 85\% \text{ of capacity break-even point.}$$

11
BUDGETING

Budgeting is planning. In order to be successful and to make meaningful decisions about the future, you must look ahead. One way to look ahead is to prepare budgets or forecasts.

A forecast may be very simple. It may be no more than estimating tomorrow's business in, for example, a restaurant, so that sufficient employees can be notified today that they are required to work tomorrow, and for how many hours.

On the other hand, a forecast of cash flow for a proposed new business may be calculated for as far ahead as five years or more.

a. PURPOSES AND ADVANTAGES OF BUDGETING

The main purposes of budgeting are to provide:

(a) Organized estimates of such things as future sales, expenses, labor requirements, and fixture and equipment needs, broken down by time period

(b) A co-ordinated management policy, both long term and short term, expressed primarily in an accounting format

(c) A method of control so that actual results can be evaluated against budget plans and adjustment, if necessary, can be made

1. Advantages of budgeting

Although there are some obvious disadvantages to budgeting, such as the time and cost involved and the difficulty in predicting the future, most business people agree that the disadvantages are far outweighed by the advantages. Some of these advantages are the following:

(a) If key employees in the business are involved in budget preparation, it encourages motivation and improves communication. These key employees can then better identify with the business's plans and objectives.

(b) Those involved in budget preparation are required to consider alternative courses of action (e.g., what if the sales forecast does not reach the budgeted level?).

(c) Operating budgets outline in advance the sales to be achieved and the costs involved with achieving those sales. Therefore, at the end of each budget period actual results can be compared with the budget. In other words, a standard for comparison is predetermined against which actual results can be evaluated.

(d) Budgeting forces those involved to look ahead. This does not mean that what happened in the past is not important for budget preparation. However, budgets are aimed at the future and require you to consider possibilities such as price changes, increasing labor and other costs, and the competition's plans.

b. PREPARING THE BUDGET

Budgets can be either long term or short term. Long-term budgets are sometimes referred to as strategic ones and are for periods of one to five years. These budgets concern matters such as business expansion, creation of a new market, and financing. From long-term plans policies evolve concerning the day-to-day operations of the business, and thus the short-term budgets.

Short-term budgets could be for a day, a week, a quarter, or a year, or for any period less than a year. Short-term budgets involve using the business' resources to meet the objectives of the long-term plans.

Although there are several different types of both long-term and short-term budgets this chapter is concerned only with the operating budget for periods up to one year ahead. The operating budget is concerned with the ongoing projections of sales and expenses, or items that affect the income statement.

The budget period normally coincides with the income statement period. For example, if the company's fiscal year is the same as the calendar one, and its income statement is prepared annually at the end of the year, its budgeted income statement would be prepared in advance of that same year.

1. Who prepares the budget?

In an owner-operated business, the owner would prepare the budget. The owner might just have a plan in mind about the future and operate from day to day to achieve this objective, or come as close to it as possible. If it were a formal budget, the help of an accountant might be useful in putting figures onto paper and refining them until the budget seems realistic.

In a larger business, a number of individuals (e.g., department heads) might be involved in budget preparation. These department heads might well, in turn, discuss the budget figures with employees within their own departments.

For the most part, short-term operating budgets are prepared annually with monthly projections. Each month, budgets for the remaining months of the year should be revised to adjust for any changed circumstances. Department heads should be involved in these revisions.

c. THE BUDGETED INCOME STATEMENT

1. Sales goals and objectives

The first step in preparing the budgeted income statement is establishing attainable sales goals or objectives. When you set your goals, you must be realistic. In other words, if there are any factors present that limit sales to a certain maximum level, these factors must not be ignored.

For example, a manufacturing plant cannot achieve more than a 100% capacity level. In the short run, sales can only be increased by increasing prices. But since few businesses do run at 100% year-round it would be unwise, desirable as it might be, to use 100% as the budgeted capacity on an annual basis.

Another limiting factor might be a lack of skilled labor or skilled supervisory personnel. Well-trained employees, or employees who could be trained, are often not available. Similarly, supervisory personnel who could train others are not always available.

Management policy can also be a limiting consideration. For example, in a restaurant, the manager may suggest that catering to bus tour groups would help increase sales. But if the owner feels that such groups would be too disruptive to the regular clientele, this market for increasing restaurant sales is not available.

Finally, customer demand and competition must be kept in mind when budgeting. In the short run there is a limited amount of business to go around. Increasing the capacity of a factory, or adding to the inventory of a retail clothing store, does not by itself increase the demand for the product. It takes time for demand to catch up with supply and new businesses, or additions to existing businesses, will usually operate at a lower level of sales than desired until additional demand increases with time.

2. Preparing income statements

The starting point in the income statement budget is estimating the sales while keeping the limiting factors in mind. Although budgeted income statements are generally prepared for one year at a time, it would be helpful for any business if they were prepared monthly (with revisions, if necessary, during the budget year). Monthly income statements are necessary so that comparison with actual results can be made each month. If comparison between budget and actual were only made on a yearly basis, any required corrective action might happen 11 months too late.

How do you set about preparing a sales forecast for a small business? If you are already in business, look first at past actual sales and trends. This analysis will answer questions such as the following:

- For each product, how much did I sell?
- For a customer class, who am I selling to?
- For a territory, where were the products sold?
- For a market, how much did each type or class of customer buy?
- What is the past and anticipated trend of sales by product, customer, territory and/or market?

The answers to these questions can usually be found in either the sales records, or the inventory records, or both. If you can't find the answers, then your accounting records need to be changed to provide you with this information.

Electronic sales registers can often be programmed to provide this data if you first define what you want. Remember, however, not to try to program the production of too much data so that you are overwhelmed with reams of useless or overly complex information.

3. External factors

In making your sales forecast, you might also need to consider the following external factors:

- Holiday or seasonal periods
- Special events
- Population changes

- Political events
- Strikes
- Inflation and similar economic factors
- Consumer earnings
- Weather
- Fashion or style changes
- Competition
- Limiting factors

4. Internal factors

Also, there could be internal factors that you should consider, such as the following:

- Advertising and promotion that you plan
- Changes in policies, such as those for credit or distribution
- Product style or quality changes
- Service type or quality changes
- Price changes
- Possible inventory or production restrictions
- Working capital problems (see next chapter)
- Labor problems

Of course, it would be impossible to build all of these factors into making precise forecasts of your sales, but this list should alert you to the many factors that you must keep in mind so that you use the most critical or likely ones to refine your sales budget.

The January sales for Betty's Books Inc. for the past three years were:

1994	$30,000
1995	35,000
1996	37,000

It is now December, 1996 and Betty is completing her budget for 1997, commencing with January. The increase in sales for year 1995 over 1994 was about 17% ($5,000 ÷ $30,000). The 1996 increase over year 1995 was approximately 6%. These increases were caused entirely by increases in demand for Betty's products.

Prices have not changed in the past three years. No expansion of Betty's sales premises will occur in 1997. Because a new competitive business, Bart's Books, is being opened close by, Betty does not anticipate that sales will increase in January, but neither does she expect to lose any of her current customers. Because of economic trends, she is forced to meet rising costs by increasing prices by 10% in January, 1997. The budgeted sales for January, 1997 would therefore be $37,000 + (10% x $37,000) = $40,700. The same type of reasoning would be applied for each of the other 11 months of 1997.

5. Deduct your operating expenses

Once forecast sales have been calculated, operating expenses that generally depend on sales (i.e., the variable costs) can be calculated and deducted.

Historic accounting records will generally show that these variable costs vary within narrow limits as a percentage of sales. The appropriate percentage figure can therefore be applied to the budgeted sales in order to calculate the dollar amount of the expense. For example, if supplies expense varies between 4½% and 5½% of sales, and sales are expected to be $100,000, the supplies expense for that period would be 5% x $100,000 = $5,000.

Similar calculations would be made for all other variable expenses. As you can no see, a break down of costs into their fixed and variable elements is very useful in budgeting. Once variable expenses have been calculated and deducted from sales, the fixed expenses can then be deducted.

Sometimes these fixed expenses will vary at the discretion of the owner or manager. For example, you may decide that a special allocation will be added to the advertising and promotion budget during the coming year or that a particular item of expensive maintenance can be deferred for a year.

Usually, these fixed expenses are estimated on an annual basis (unlike sales and variable expenses, which are generally calculated monthly). The simplest method of allocating these fixed expenses by month is to show one-twelfth of the annual expense as a monthly cost.

6. Comparing your results

Comparing actual results with those planned or budgeted is probably the most important and advantageous step in the budgeting process. Comparing actual with budget allows you to examine reasons for differences. For example, if actual sales in April were $30,000 instead of the budgeted $33,000, was the difference caused by a reduction in number of customers? If so, is there an explanation? For example, are higher prices keeping customers away, or did a competitive business open nearby?

These are just some examples of the types of questions that can be asked when you analyze differences between budgeted and actual performance.

7. Corrective action

The next step in the budget process requires you to take corrective action (if this is required) because of differences between budgeted and actual figures.

The difference could be caused by an unforeseen circumstance (e.g., weather, a sudden change in economic conditions, a fire on the premises). On the other hand, a difference could be caused by failure to increase prices sufficiently to compensate for inflationary cost increases or to adjust the sales forecast to compensate for the opening of a new, nearby competitive business.

Whatever the reason, it should be corrected if possible so that future budgets can more realistically predict planned operation.

8. Improve your budget effectiveness

The final step in the budgeting process is a continual effort to try to improve the budgeting process. The information provided from past budgets, particularly the information provided by analyzing differences between actual and budgeted figures, will be helpful. By improving accuracy in budgeting, the effectiveness of your business's operation will improve.

d. BUDGETING IN A NEW BUSINESS

Owners of new businesses will find it more difficult to budget in their early years since they have no internal historic information to serve as a base. If a feasibility study has been prepared prior to opening, it could serve as a base for budgeting. Alternatively, forecasts must be founded on a combination of known facts and industry or market averages for that type and size of business.

Some of the sources of information for a new business might be —

- Chamber of commerce or Board of Trade
- City or municipal hall
- Local (federal or state/provincial) government offices
- Local business or trade associations
- Shopping center developers
- Media, such as newspapers, and radio and TV stations

- Possible competitors
- Trade publications
- Businesses in the neighborhood where you plan to locate
- Sales people
- Trade suppliers

Once you have contacted as many likely sources as possible to obtain information about possible sales levels and cost information, you can then prepare your budgeted income statement. Your first try may not be as close to actual as you would like, but once you have gone through the first actual cycle of business you can improve your budgeting effectiveness from then on by following the steps outlined in this chapter.

12
CASH MANAGEMENT

You will remember from chapter 3 that, listed under the assets on the balance sheet, is a section called current assets. This includes items such as cash, accounts receivable, marketable securities, inventories, and prepaid expenses. Current assets are generally considered to be items that are cash, or can be converted into cash fairly quickly or in less than a year if necessary.

On the other side of the balance sheet is a section for the current liabilities for such items as accounts payable, accrued expenses, income tax payable, current portion of long-term mortgages, and dividends payable. Current liabilities are debts that have to be paid within the next year. They are generally paid by the cash that normally circulates through a business.

This circulation results from using cash to buy inventory, selling that inventory for cash or on credit (accounts receivable) and collecting cash from the accounts receivable. Since the selling price of items purchased for inventory is greater than their cost, a "profit" results, and thus current assets can be used to pay for current liabilities.

However, it is not always that simple. The ability of a business to pay its current liabilities when they are due depends on the amount and timing of cash inflows from cash and credit sales. As long as most sales are for cash, or if credit sales are collected quickly, then there should be sufficient cash to pay for current liabilities. But if you are overstocked with inventory or find it difficult to collect on accounts receivable, cash flow may be troublesome.

The difference between total current assets and total current liabilities is known as working capital: Current assets - current liabilities = working capital.

However, even though working capital is defined as the arithmetical difference between current assets and current liabilities, it is, more importantly, a reflection of the ability of the manager of the business to effectively control each current asset and current liability account given the operating conditions for that business.

In other words, the amount of working capital required by a business is the amount that results from each current asset and each current liability being at the best level to ensure, for example, that there is sufficient inventory on hand, or that accounts payable are paid when due.

A business with a good working capital position will be able to buy its inventory, supplies, and services on favorable terms and with satisfactory delivery schedules. It will be able to take advantage of trade discounts offered and keep its own prices competitive. It will have a good credit rating and will not be dictated to by its creditors. It will collect accounts receivable promptly and not suffer high bad debt losses.

Money does not always come into a business at the same rate it goes out. At times there will be excess cash on hand, at other times there will be shortages of cash. You need to anticipate both of these events so that shortages can be covered. In this way the cash balance will be kept at its optimum level.

For example, many retail sales businesses, prior to certain peak sales periods, have to borrow large amounts of money to build up their inventories and tie up working capital prior to the sale of the products. After the peak sale they may have surplus cash available for a few months prior to the next peak sales period. In such a situation the peaks and valleys must be fairly accurately forecast.

One of the ways to do this is to be familiar with and properly manage your various working capital accounts. Good management of working capital will help you generate a good deal of internal financing for your business.

a. HOW MUCH WORKING CAPITAL?

How much working capital does a business need? This cannot be answered with an absolute dollar amount.

For example, suppose it were a rule of thumb that a business should have a working capital of $5,000. A business might find itself with the following:

Current assets	$15,000
Current liabilities	10,000
Working capital	$ 5,000

A larger business would have to have larger amounts of cash, inventories, accounts receivable, and other items that are current assets. Also, it would probably have larger amounts in its various current liability accounts. Its balance sheet might therefore look like this:

Current assets	$100,000
Current liabilities	95,000
Working capital	$ 5,000

The smaller business is in much better financial shape than the larger one. The former has $1.50 ($15,000 ÷ $10,000) of current assets for every $1.00 of current liabilities — a comfortable cushion. The latter has just over $1.05 ($100,000 ÷ 95,000) of current assets for each dollar of current liabilities — not so comfortable a cushion.

A general rule in business is that a company should preferably have at least $2 of current assets for each $1 of current liabilities. This would mean that its working capital ($2 - $1) is equivalent to its current liabilities.

However, this rule is primarily for companies that need to carry very large inventories that do not turn over very rapidly (such as manufacturing, wholesaling, and some retailing organizations).

Other businesses can operate with a very low ratio of current assets to current liabilities — often as low as 1 to 1. In other words, for each $1 of current assets there is $1 of current liabilities. This means that the business has, in fact, no net working capital.

At certain times of the year, some businesses can even operate with negative working capital. In other words, current liabilities will exceed current assets. This might be typical of a business that is seasonal in nature. Such an operation would have current assets vastly in excess of current liabilities during the peak season, but the reverse situation could prevail in the off season.

b. CASH

Cash on hand, as distinguished from cash in the bank, is the money in circulation in a business. This could be cash used by cashiers as "floats" or "banks" for change, petty cash, or just general cash in the safe. The amount of cash on hand should be sufficient for normal day-to-day operations only. Any surplus idle cash should be deposited in the bank in savings accounts or term deposits so that it can earn interest. Preferably, each day's net cash receipts should be deposited in the bank as soon as possible the following day.

Cash in the bank in the current account should be sufficient to pay only current bills due or current payroll. Any excess funds should be invested in short-term securities or in savings or other special accounts that earn interest. It may please your bank manager to leave these excess funds in your current account, rather than earn interest on them, but that is not a good business practice.

c. ACCOUNTS RECEIVABLE

Extending credit to your customers is a useful marketing tool to encourage increased sales. However, to maximize this potential you must establish credit policies to ensure your credit system is not so loose that it costs you cash and thus profit.

1. Terms of credit

You need to decide who will be allowed credit and how to determine a customer's credit limit. You also need to decide who has authority to decide who may receive credit and up to what limits. In other words, up to what amount can a customer charge items purchased before credit is no longer extended?

Your terms of credit must also be spelled out for your customers. For example, if you offer a discount off the purchase price for prompt payment of an invoice, what are the discount terms? Also, if full payment is to be made within, let us say, 30 days, is this 30 days from the date of purchase, date of mailing of the invoice, the end of the month following the customer's receipt of the invoice, or some other alternative?

You should make clear to the customer when you expect payment and when you will begin to implement some follow-up procedure. If you don't do this, you may soon find your cost of extending credit is climbing steeply.

For example, suppose with a 30-day credit limit after purchase of goods your normal balance of accounts receivable is $50,000. If all your customers stretch this to 60 days, your accounts receivable balance will increase to $100,000. That extra $50,000 of credit at a 15% interest rate will increase your cost of doing business by $7,500 a year.

High credit standards can lead to loss of revenue. On the other hand, low standards can lead to bad debts and collection costs.

2. Two areas

Pay attention to two areas of your accounts receivable: ensure that invoices are mailed out promptly and follow up on delinquent accounts to have them collected. Money tied up in accounts receivable is money not earning a return.

Extension of credit to customers is an accepted form of business transaction, but it should not be extended to the point of allowing payments to lag two or three months behind the mailing of the invoice.

A couple of methods of keeping an eye on accounts receivable were discussed in chapter 6. Another way of keeping an eye on the accounts receivable in a business is to periodically (once a month) prepare a chart showing the age of the accounts outstanding. (See Sample #20.)

Sample #20 shows that the accounts receivable outstanding situation has not improved from May to June. In May, 79.5% of total receivables were less than 30 days old. In June only 74.2% were less than 30 days outstanding. Similarly, the relative percentages in the 31- to 60-day category has worsened from May to June. By contrast, in the 61- to 90-day bracket, 11.3% of accounts receivable are outstanding in June, against only 3.2% in May.

This particular aging chart shows that the accounts receivable are getting older. If this trend continues, the business should improve its collection procedures. If, after all possible collection procedures have been explored, the account is deemed to be uncollectible (a bad debt), it would then be removed from the accounts receivable and recorded as a bad debt expense. The decision on its uncollectibility should be made by the owner or manager.

3. Credit cards

Most retail businesses these days accept a variety of credit cards for payment of purchases. You should train your employees to follow established procedures to eliminate losses from matters such as customers purchasing in an amount above their credit card limit, or using stolen or blacklisted credit cards.

Commissions paid to credit card companies can range as high as 6% of your sales on the commercial credit cards (American Express and Diners Club) whereas the commission rate is considerably less on the bank credit cards (Visa and MasterCard). You will also receive the cash from bank credit card sales vouchers the day you deposit them in the bank.

With commercial credit cards, even if you mail the vouchers promptly you might wait two weeks or more before receiving a payment. Your employees should therefore be trained to encourage customers to use bank credit cards rather than commercial ones wherever possible. This will help maximize your profits.

SAMPLE #20
ACCOUNTS RECEIVABLE CHART

AGE	MAY 31		JUNE 30	
0 - 30 days	$59,000	79.5%	$56,400	74.2%
31-60 days	11,800	15.9	8,800	11.6
61-90 days	2,400	3.2	8,600	11.3
over 90 days	1,000	1.4	2,200	2.9
Totals	$74,200	100.0	$76,000	100.0

4. Lockboxes

If the volume of your credit sales is large enough, you might also want to consider using a lockbox. With a lockbox you do not directly collect your own receivables. Instead, customers are directed to send their payment of accounts to a post office box number. Mail from this box is picked up by your bank and the deposits put immediately into your bank account. The bank notifies you each day of the amounts deposited so that you can adjust your accounts receivable records.

The main advantage of the lockbox system is that you gain a day or two on outstanding receivables (and can earn interest on this money).

However, there is a bank cost for using this system, usually in the form of a charge for each receivable check handled. You will need to discuss with your bank manager whether the cost of a lockbox system for your business will exceed the benefits.

5. Deposits

In some businesses it is possible to encourage customers to make payment, or partial payment, by deposit prior to production or delivery of the goods. In other situations, the customer will make payment in stages as work progresses. This reduces the amount that you will be carrying in receivables. In other words, it helps you finance your business and improve your cash flow.

Mail order businesses, customer manufacturers, and building contractors typically require the customer to pay part or all of the purchase price in advance.

d. MARKETABLE SECURITIES

Generally, a business should invest any surplus cash not needed in the short-run in some type of marketable security. This investment could be for a few days, but generally is for longer periods such as 30, 60, or 90 days, or even, under certain circumstances, for up to a year.

Most businesses, particularly if their trade is seasonal, will have peaks and valleys in their cash flows and the cash surpluses from peak periods should be invested until needed during slow sales periods.

1. Risk versus liquidity

The two main factors you must consider in investing in marketable securities are risk and liquidity. A low-risk investment generally yields a lower interest rate. Most government securities offer a very low risk and can generally be cashed in at any time at face value without loss of interest. However, such securities sometimes have a lower interest rate than, for example, bank term deposits or similar investments.

In certain cases a business might consider investing in the stocks and/or bonds offered by larger public companies through the various stock exchanges. The returns on these security investments can sometimes be quite high, but there is also a relatively high risk; a small business should only invest surplus cash in them with caution.

It might be a good idea to consult with your banker, or other investment advisor, to decide what is the best type of investment at any particular time for any surplus cash your business has.

e. INVENTORY

For most small businesses inventory control is critical. Inventory control requires establishing a system for ensuring that goods received are checked off against invoices, that they are stored until needed or sold, and that production or sales controls are in effect to minimize losses from inventory.

However, from an overall financial management point of view, it is just as important to ensure that only the right amount of inventory is carried at any one time so that there is

104

neither an over- nor an under-investment in inventory. Inventory turnover is one way of doing this (see chapter 6 for a definition of inventory turnover).

1. Inventory turnover

Generally, the higher the turnover rate, the lower the amount of money invested in inventory, and vice versa. The inventory turnover rate can vary widely from one type of business to another, and even for businesses of the same type, although average figures for various types of business can be determined.

You should try to find out the most appropriate level of turnover for your business to avoid having too little or too much inventory. Watch for deviations from that level.

Some businesses may have several different types of inventory. For example, a manufacturing company will probably have inventories for raw materials, goods in progress, finished goods, parts, and supplies. In such cases it is a good idea to calculate inventory turnover for each type of inventory.

2. Number of days inventory

In other cases inventory turnover may not be the most appropriate measure for determining the right amount of inventory to carry. An alternative might be to value it in terms of a number-of-days' purchases or a number-of-days' sales.

For example, if inventory is worth $25,000 and represents about 25 days of sales and a "safe" level of inventory is to have only about 20 days' sales on hand, inventory could be safely reduced by $5,000. This type of evaluation is useful if sales are budgeted month by month and tend to be cyclical or seasonal. Inventory can then be adjusted up or down each month in line with projected sales.

This type of inventory adjustment requires keeping a close eye on purchases and delivery times and possible delays, as well as on likely sales demand if inventory comprises a variety of different products.

Since customers generally expect you to have on hand what they want at the time they want it, you must be familiar with both the slow and the fast moving items, and which items you can purchase on short notice to keep inventory at a minimum without risk of running out.

If your business is still growing, or is planning an expansion, then you must, ahead of time, calculate the increased inventory required based on past experience. The funds for purchasing and holding this increased inventory must also be planned.

f. COMPOSITION OF CURRENT ASSETS

Some current assets are more "liquid" than others. For example, cash is more liquid than accounts receivable. The more liquid the current assets are the better it is under normal circumstances. One useful method of assessing a change in current asset liquidity is to make a periodic (e.g., monthly) breakdown of your current assets.

To do this, total current assets for the period are given a value of 100%, and each of the current assets is then expressed as a fraction of 100. This is illustrated as follows:

	Month 1		Month 2	
Cash	$ 45,800	28.3%	$ 70,800	40.5%
Marketable securities	30,000	18.5	4,000	2.3
Accounts receivable	46,200	28.6	50,400	28.9
Inventory	39,800	24.6	49,400	28.3
Totals	$161,800	100.0%	$174,600	100.0%

The above figures show that cash represented 28.3% of total current assets in month 1 and 40.5% in month 2. At the same time, investment in marketable securities declined from 18.5% to 2.3%. Obviously most of the marketable securities have been converted into cash. Was there a good reason for this?

The total of the most liquid current assets (cash and marketable securities) declined from 46.8% (28.3% + 18.5%) to 42.8% (40.5% + 2.3%). This would not normally be a desirable trend.

Little change occurred in accounts receivable. If a major change did take place, reference to the aging schedule for the relevant months would possibly explain the reason.

Finally, the amount in inventory increased from 24.6% to 28.3%. This is a relatively large shift and reference to the inventory turnover ratios or days sales tied up inventory might offer an explanation.

g. ACCOUNTS PAYABLE

So far in this chapter, methods of managing current assets to conserve cash have been discussed. However, you should not overlook your current liabilities (such as accounts payable) since cash savings can also be made there.

1. Timing of purchases and payments

Wherever possible, you should take advantage of a supplier's billing practices. Most companies supply goods as required during a month and within a few days of the month end mail a statement for that month to you.

Suppose you buy a month's supply of items from a supplier at the beginning of each month, using the items as required during the month and that the terms on the supplier's month end statement are "2/10, net 30." This means there is a 2% discount off the total month's purchases if the statement is paid within 10 days of the month end; otherwise the statement is payable within 30 days without discount.

You thus have the use of the supplier's credit for 40 days if you take advantage of the discount, otherwise for 60 days. In other words, you can use this "free" money to advantage, even if all you do is collect bank interest on it.

On the other hand, suppose you purchase from the same supplier, but habitually buy at the end of each month sufficient goods to carry you through until the end of the next month. In this case you will have the use of the "free" money for only 10 days, if you take advantage of the discount, and otherwise only for 30 days.

These two cases are extreme, but they do point out that wise purchasing can take advantage of a supplier's billing practices in order to increase your profits.

2. Purchase discounts

Whenever a purchase discount is offered, you should consider taking it. For example, suppose the terms are 2/10, net 60. On a $5,000 purchase paid within 10 days this would save $100 (2% x $5,000). This can amount to a considerable sum if it is made on all similar purchases made during a year.

However, in the example given, you may have to borrow the money ($4,900) in order to make the payment within 10 days. Let us assume the money is borrowed for 50 days (60 days less 10 days) at a 10% interest rate. The interest expense on this borrowed money is —

$$\frac{\$4,900 \times 50 \text{ days} \times 10\%}{365 \text{ days}} = \$67.12$$

In this case it would be advantageous to borrow the money since the discount saving of $100.00 is greater than the interest expense of $67.12.

3. Deferring payments until due

Whether you take a discount or not, it is a good idea to hold on to your money (and earn interest on it) until payments are due. This does not mean delaying payments until they are delinquent since a business with a reputation for delinquency may find it has difficulty obtaining goods, supplies, and services on anything but a cash basis.

Rather it means taking advantage of a supplier's trade credit terms until the supplier expects you to pay the bill. (The use of trade credit as a form of equity financing will be discussed in more depth in chapter 17).

4. Using bank float

Another good idea for conserving cash in paying accounts is the use of bank float. A float is the difference between the bank balance shown on your records and the balance of actual cash in the bank.

This difference exists because it takes time (because of mail processing and the handling and depositing of your check by the receiver) between the moment you write a check and the moment it is deducted by your bank from your account. Since this time can be a day or two, or even longer over a weekend, you can leave that amount of surplus cash in an account bearing interest until it is needed in your current account to cover checks written and in transit.

h. PROFIT IS NOT CASH

Many small businesses make a profit according to their income statement, but don't have the cash to pay their current accounts payable. A business will not exist for long if it does not pay its bills. Cash management is, therefore, an extremely important part of the financial management of any small business.

Even though it is better to have too much rather than not enough cash, it is better still to have just the right amount. The objective of cash management is to determine what that correct amount is so that any surplus cash can be used to increase profits.

One of the most important facts you must remember in managing cash and analyzing income statements is that the net profit amount shown on the income statement is not the equivalent of cash. A reason for this is the accrual nature of the accounting process (discussed in chapter 2).

With accrual accounting, sales are recorded at the time the sale is made, even though the payment of cash for the sale might not be received until some time later.

For example, if you sell $100 worth of goods on January 15 and are paid cash at the time of the sale, the $100 will be recorded as a sale on your income statement for January and will also show as a cash receipt on your January cash flow statement.

However, if you sell $100 worth of goods on January 15 on 30-day terms and don't receive the cash until February 15, this will be recorded as a sale on your January income statement but will only show as a cash receipt on your February cash flow statement. Similarly, you can purchase supplies on credit. In other words, the goods are received and used but not paid for until at least 30 days later. However, as long as the goods are used during the income statement period, they are recorded on the income statement as an expense.

Also, some expenses may be prepaid at the beginning of the year (e.g., insurance expense) yet the total insurance cost is spread equally over each monthly income statement for the entire year. This means that, for example, in January $12,000 might be paid out for annual insurance, yet only $1,000 is recorded on the January income statement as an expense, and $1,000 will be shown as an expense for each of the next 11 months.

Another complicating factor is that some items, such as depreciation, are recorded as an expense on the income statements even though no cash is involved.

If you wish to equate net income with cash (a good idea in most businesses), you must convert it to a cash basis, and one of the ways to do this is to prepare cash budgets. Cash budgets are a major aid in effective cash management.

i. CASH BUDGETS

The starting point in cash budgeting is the budgeted income statement showing the anticipated (forecast) sales and expenses by month for as long a period as is required for cash budget preparation.

In this case we will use a three-month period. The budgeted income statements for the next quarter of Bee's Business are shown in Sample #21.

In order to prepare a cash budget for Bee's Business, we need some additional information.

(a) Accounting records show that, each month, approximately 60% of the sales are in the form of cash, and 40% are on credit and collected the following month.

(b) December sales were $56,000 (we need this information so that we can calculate the amount of cash that is going to be collected in January from sales made in December).

(c) Wages, supplies, utilities, and rent are paid 100% cash during each current month.

(d) Advertising has been prepaid in December ($12,000) for the entire current year. In order not to show the full $12,000 as an expense in January (since the benefit of the advertising is for a full year), the income statements show $1,000 each month for this prepaid expense.

(e) The bank balance on January 1 is $20,400.

We can now use the budgeted income statements in Sample #21 and the above information to calculate the figures for the cash budget. The process is simple. The first cash budget month is January. The cash receipts for January are —

(a) Current month sales $60,000 x 60% cash = $36,000

(b) Accounts receivable collections, December sales: $56,000 x 40% = $22,400.

The cash disbursements for January are —

(a) Wages, 100% cash = $42,000

(b) Supplies, 100% cash = $3,000

(c) Utilities, 100% cash = $1,000

(d) Rent, 100% cash = $2,000

(e) Advertising was paid in December for the entire current year so the full $12,000 would have been recorded as a cash disbursement at that time. Therefore the cash amount for January = 0

(f) Depreciation does not require a disbursement of cash; it is simply a write-down of the book value of the related asset(s).

The completed cash budget for the month of January would then be as follows:

Opening bank balance	$20,400
Receipts:	
Cash sales	36,000
Collections on account	22,400
Total	$78,800
Disbursements:	
Wages	$42,000
Supplies	3,000
Utilities	1,000
Rent	2,000
Total	$48,000
Closing bank balance	$30,800

Note that the closing bank balance each month is calculated as: opening bank balance + receipts - disbursements = closing bank balance.

Each month the closing bank balance becomes the opening bank balance of the following month. The completed cash budget for the three-month period is shown in Sample #22. This sample shows that the bank account is expected to increase from $20,400 to $52,800 over the next three months. When the cash budget for the months of April, May, and June is prepared, it will show whether or not the bank balance is going to continue to increase or start to decline.

This sample cash budget shows that in Bee's Business there is going to be a fairly healthy surplus of cash (as long as budget projections are reasonably accurate) that should not be left to accumulate at no or low interest in a bank account. Bee might want to take $40,000 or $50,000 out of the bank account and invest it in high interest rate short-term (30-, 60-, or 90-day) securities.

Without a cash budget, Bee would not have known that she will have surplus funds on hand to use for increasing net profit and cash receipts. If the cash is taken out of the bank account and invested, the cash budget has to show this as a disbursement until the securities are cashed in and shown as a receipt.

Similarly, interest on loans, principal payments on loans, purchases of fixed assets, income tax payments, and dividend payouts are also recorded on the cash budget as disbursements. If any fixed assets are sold for cash, the cash received shows as a receipt.

j. NEGATIVE CASH BUDGETS

Seasonal businesses may find that for some months of the year their disbursements exceed receipts to the point that they have negative cash budgets.

However, by preparing a cash budget ahead of time, the business can show that is has anticipated the cash shortage and can plan to cover it with, for example, a short-term bank loan. Such a loan will be easier to obtain when the banker sees that good cash management is being practiced through the preparation of a cash budget.

Any loans received to cover cash shortages should be recorded as receipts on the cash budget at that time, and as disbursements when paid back.

The cash budget, particularly if prepared a year ahead, can help you not only in making decisions about investing excess funds and arranging to borrow funds to cover shortages, but also in making discretionary decisions concerning such things as major renovations, replacement of fixed assets, and payment of dividends.

SAMPLE #21
BUDGETED INCOME STATEMENT

	January		February		March	
Sales		$60,000		$70,000		$80,000
Wages	$42,000		$49,000		$56,000	
Supplies	3,000		3,500		4,000	
Utilities	1,000		1,500		2,000	
Rent	2,000		2,000		2,000	
Advertising	1,000		1,000		1,000	
Depreciation	4,000	53,000	4,000	61,000	4,000	69,000
Net profit		$ 7,000		$ 9,000		$11,000

115

SAMPLE #22
CASH BUDGET

	January	February	March
Opening bank balance	$20,400	$30,800	$ 40,800
Receipts:			
Cash sales	36,000	42,000	48,000
Accounts receivable (collections)	22,400	24,000	28,000
	$78,800	$96,800	$116,800
Disbursements:			
Wages	$42,000	$49,000	$ 56,000
Supplies	3,000	3,500	4,000
Utilities	1,000	1,500	2,000
Rent	2,000	2,000	2,000
Totals	$48,000	$56,000	$ 64,000
Closing bank balance	$30,800	$40,800	$ 52,800

116

13
LONG-TERM INVESTMENTS

The money you invest in your small business may be needed to buy fixed or long-term assets. This type of asset is needed to operate the business and is not sold as are products. Included in long-term assets are land, building, equipment and fixtures, and vehicles.

A part of the useful life of each kind of long-term asset (except land) is used up over time as you sell your products and/or services. In other words, most fixed assets generally wear out or deteriorate over time.

The initial value of long-term assets recorded on the balance sheet is the cost or price originally paid. In each income statement period (month, quarter, or year), a part of this cost is deducted from the original cost on the balance sheet and is shown as an expense on the income statement. This expense is normally called depreciation. Investment in long-term assets is sometimes referred to as capital budgeting, but we are not so much concerned in this chapter with the budgeting process as we are with the decision about whether or not to make a specific investment, or with the decision about which of two or more investments would be preferable.

The largest investment that some businesses have is in their land and building. This is a one-time investment for each separate property. However, this chapter is primarily concerned about more frequent investment decisions for items such as equipment and fixtures purchase and replacement.

Long-term investment decision making differs from day-to-day decision making and ongoing budgeting in a number of ways. For example, long-term investment decisions concern assets that have a relatively long life. Day-to-day decisions concern assets that turn over frequently. A wrong decision about a piece of equipment can have an effect for many years. A wrong decision about operating supplies has only a short-run effect.

Also, day-to-day operating decisions do not usually involve large amounts of money for any individual item, whereas the purchase of a long-term asset requires the outlay of a large sum of money that can have a major effect if a wrong decision is made.

Four methods of investment decision making that you can use are the following:

(a) Average rate of return (ARR)

(b) Payback period

(c) Net present value (NPV)

(d) Internal rate of return (IRR)

To set the scene for the average rate of return and the payback period methods, consider Wally's wholesale business, which uses a hand system for recording sales. Wally is investigating the value of installing an electronic register that will eliminate part of the present wage cost and save an estimated $4,000 a year. The register will cost $5,000 and is expected to have a five-year life with no trade-in value. Depreciation is therefore $1,000 a year ($5,000 ÷ 5). Savings and expense figures are —

Savings: — Employee wages	<u>$4,000</u>
Expenses:	
Maintenance	$ 350
Stationery	650

Depreciation	<u>1,000</u>
Total	<u>$2,000</u>
Savings before tax	$2,000
Income tax	<u>1,000</u>
Net annual savings	<u>$1,000</u>

a. AVERAGE RATE OF RETURN

The average rate of return method compares the average annual net profit (after income tax) resulting from the investment with the average investment. The formula is —

$$\text{Average rate of return (ARR)} = \frac{\text{Net annual saving}}{\text{Average investment}}$$

Note that the average investment is, simply, initial investment divided by two. Using the information from above, the ARR is —

$$\frac{\$1,000}{\$2,500\ \$(5,000/\ 2)} \times 100 = 40.0\%$$

The advantage of the average rate of return method is its simplicity. It is frequently used to compare the anticipated return from a proposal with a minimum desired return. If the proposal's return is less than desired, it is rejected. If greater than desired, a more indepth analysis, using other investment techniques, might then be used.

The major disadvantage of the ARR is that it is based on net profit rather than on cash flow.

b. PAYBACK PERIOD

The payback period method overcomes the cash flow shortcoming of the ARR. The payback method measures the initial investment with the annual cash inflows. The equation is —

$$\text{Payback period} = \frac{\text{Initial investment}}{\text{Net annual cash savings}}$$

Since the information above only gives net annual savings, and not net annual cash savings, we must first convert the net annual savings figure to a cash basis. This is done by adding back the depreciation (an expense that does not require an outlay of cash). The cash savings figure is —

Net annual savings	$1,000
Add depreciation	1,000
Net annual cash savings	$2,000

The payback period is then:

$$\frac{\$5,000}{\$2,000} = 2.5 \text{ years}$$

The payback period method, although simple, does not really measure the merits of investments, but only the speed with which the investment cost might be recovered. It has a use in evaluating a number of proposals so that only those that fall within a predetermined payback period will be considered for further evaluation using other investment techniques.

However, both the payback period and the ARR methods still suffer from a common fault: they both ignore the time value of cash flows, or the concept that money now is worth more than the same amount of money at some time in the future. This concept is discussed in the next section, after which we will explore the use of the net present value and internal rate of return methods.

c. DISCOUNTED CASH FLOW

The concept of discounted cash flow can probably best be understood by looking first at an example of compound interest. Table #3 shows, year by year, what happens to $100 invested at a 10% compound interest rate. At the end of four years, the investment would be worth $146.41.

120

Discounting is simply the reverse of compounding interest. In other words, at a 10% interest rate, what is $146.41 four years from now worth today? The solution could be worked out manually or with a hand calculator, but can much more easily be solved by using a table of discounted cash flow factors (see Table #4).

In Table #4, look at the number, called a factor, that is opposite year 4 and under the 10% column; you will see that it is 0.6830. This factor tells us that $1 received at the end of year 4 is worth only $1 x 0.683 = $0.683 right now.

Indeed, this factor tells us, expressed in a different way, that any amount of money at the end of four years from now at a 10% interest (discount) rate is worth only 68.3% of that amount right now. You can prove this by taking the $146.41 amount at the end of year 4 from Table #3 and discounting it back to the present: $146.41 x 0.683 = $99.99803 or $100.00.

We know that $100 is the right answer because it is the amount we started with in the illustration of compounding interest in Table #3.

For a series of annual cash flows, simply apply the related annual discount factor for that year to the cash inflow for that year. For example, a cash inflow of $1,000 a year for each of three years using a 10% factor will produce the following total discounted cash flow:

YEAR	FACTOR	AMOUNT	TOTAL
1	0.9091	$1,000	$ 909.10
2	0.8264	$1,000	826.40
3	0.7513	$1,000	751.30
			$2,486.80

TABLE #3
EFFECT OF COMPOUNDING INTEREST

	Jan. 1 Year 1	Dec. 31 Year 1	Dec. 31 Year 2	Dec. 31 Year 3	Dec. 31 Year 4
Balance forward Interest 10%	$100.00	$100.00 10.00	$110.00 11.00	$121.00 12.10	$133.10 13.31
Investment value end of year		$110.00	$121.00	$133.10	$146.41

TABLE #4
DISCOUNTED CASH FLOW FACTORS

	Year 1	Year 2	Year 3	Year 4	Year 5
Wage saving	$4,000	$4,000	$4,000	$4,000	$4,000
Expenses:					
Training cost	$3,500				
Maintenance	400	$ 400	$ 400	$ 400	$ 400
Overhaul			400		
Stationery	600	600	600	600	600
Depreciation	800	800	800	800	800
Total	$5,300	$1,800	$2,200	$1,800	$1,800
Saving less expenses	($1,300)	$2,200	$1,800	$2,200	$2,200
Income tax 50%	0	1,100	900	1,100	1,100
Net savings	($1,300)	$1,100	$ 900	$1,100	$1,100
Add: depreciation	800	800	800	800	800
trade-in					1,000
Net cash flow	($ 500)	$1,900	$1,700	$1,900	$2,900

d. NET PRESENT VALUE

Discounted cash flow can be used with the net present value (NPV) method for evaluating investment proposals. Sample #23 gives projections of savings and costs for a new machine. The price of the machine is $5,000.

The estimate of the future savings and costs is the most difficult part of the exercise. In this case, you are forecasting for five years ahead. Obviously, the longer the period of time, the less accurate the estimates are likely to be. Note that depreciation is calculated as follows:

Initial cost	$5,000
Less: trade in	(1,000)
	$4,000

$$\text{Depreciation} \quad \frac{\$4,000}{5} = \$800/\text{year}$$

Also note that depreciation is deductible as an expense for the calculation of income tax, but this expense does not require an outlay of cash year by year. Therefore, in order to convert the annual net savings from the investment to a cash situation, the depreciation is added back each year.

Note also that there is a negative cash flow in year 1. The trade-in value is a partial recovery of the initial investment and is therefore added as a positive cash flow at the end of year 5.

The initial investment and the annual net cash flow figures have been transferred to Sample #24, and, using the relevant 10% discount factors from Table #4, have been converted to a net present value basis. Note how the negative cash flow has been handled.

As you can see from Sample #24, the net present value figure is positive. It is possible for a net present value figure to be negative if the initial investment exceeds the sum of the individual years' present values. In the case of negative NPV, the investment should not be undertaken because the investment will not produce the rate of return desired.

Finally, the discount rate actually used should be realistic. It is frequently the rate that the owners expect the business to earn, after taxes, on the equity investment.

e. INTERNAL RATE OF RETURN

As we have seen, the NPV method uses a specific discount rate to determine if proposals result in a net present value greater than zero. Those that do not are rejected.

The internal rate of return (IRR) method also uses the discounted cash flow concept. However, this method determines the interest (discount) rate that will make the total discounted cash inflows equal the initial investment.

For example, Belle Businesswoman decides to investigate renting a building adjacent to her business in order to increase sales. Her investigation shows that it will cost $200,000 to renovate and equip the building. If she takes a guaranteed five-year lease, the projected cash flow (net profit after tax, with depreciation added back) for each of the five years is as follows:

YEAR	CASH FLOW
1	$ 36,000
2	40,000
3	44,000
4	50,000
5	60,000
	$230,000

125

SAMPLE #23
CALCULATION OF ANNUAL NET CASH FLOWS

	Year 1	Year 2	Year 3	Year 4	Year 5
Wage saving	$4,000	$4,000	$4,000	$4,000	$4,000
Expenses:					
Training cost	$3,500				
Maintenance	400	$ 400	$ 400	$ 400	$ 400
Overhaul	400				
Stationery	600	600	600	600	600
Depreciation	800	800	800	800	
Total	$5,300	$1,800	$2,200	$1,800	$1,800
Saving less expenses	($1,300)	$2,200	$1,800	$2,200	$2,200
Income tax 50%	0	$1,100	900	1,100	1,100
Net savings	($1,300)	$1,100	$ 900	$1,100	$1,100
Add: depreciation trade-in	800	800	800	800	800 $1,000
Net cash flow	($ 500)	$1,900	$1,700	$1,900	$2,900

126

SAMPLE #24
NET PRESENT VALUE

Year	Net cash flow	Discount factor	Present value
1	($ 500)	0.9091	($ 455)
2	1,900	0.8264	1,570
3	1,700	0.7513	1,277
4	1,900	0.6830	1,298
5	2,900	0.6209	1,801
		Total present value	$5,491
		Initial investment	5,000
		Net present value	$ 491

In addition to the total of $230,000 cash recovery over the five years, Belle estimates the equipment can be sold for $20,000 at the end of the lease period. The total cash recovery is therefore $230,000 + $20,000 = $250,000, which is $50,000 more than the initial investment required of $200,000.

On the face of it, Belle seems to be ahead of the game. If the annual flows are discounted back to their net present value, however, a different pictures emerges (see Sample #25). This shows that the future flows of cash discounted back to today's values using a 12% rate is less than the initial investment by over $27,000. Thus, Belle knows that if the projections about the venture are correct, there will not be a 12% cash return on her investment.

The IRR method can be used to determine the return that will be earned if the investment is made. Belle knows that 12%

is too high. By moving to a lower rate of interest, she will eventually, by trial and error, arrive at one where the NPV (the difference between the total present value and initial investment) is virtually zero. This is illustrated in Sample #26 with a 7% interest (discount) rate.

The figures in Sample #26 tell Belle that the initial $200,000 investment will return the initial cash outlay except for about $300 and earn 7% on the investment. Or, stated slightly differently, Belle would recover the full $200,000 but earn slightly less than 7% interest. If she is satisfied with a 7% cash return on the investment (this is 7% after income tax), then she should go ahead with the project.

f. NON-QUANTIFIABLE BENEFITS

In this chapter various methods of making investment decisions have been examined. Information that is not easily quantifiable but that might still be relevant to decision making has been ignored. You should not forget factors like prestige, goodwill, reputation, employee or customer acceptance, and the social or environmental implications of investment decisions.

For example, if you redecorate your reception area, you should consider the cash benefits. They may be difficult to quantify, but to retain customer goodwill the reception area may have to be redecorated.

Similarly, how do you assess the relative benefits of spending $5,000 on reception area redecoration versus Christmas bonuses for the employees? Personal judgment must come into play in such decisions.

SAMPLE #25
NET PRESENT VALUE

Year	Annual cash flow	Discount factor 12%	Present value
1	$36,000	0.8929	$ 32,144
2	40,000	0.7972	31,888
3	44,000	0.7118	31,319
4	50,000	0.6355	31,775
5	60,000	0.5674	11,348
5	20,000 (trade-in)	0.5674	11,348
		Total present value	$172,518
		Initial investment	200,000
		Net present value	($ 27,482)

SAMPLE #26
INTERNAL RATE OF RETURN

Year	Annual cash flow	Discount factor 7%	Present value
1	$36,000	0.9346	$ 33,646
2	40,000	0.8734	34,936
3	44,000	0.8163	35,917
4	50,000	0.7629	38,145
5	60,000	0.7130	42,780
5	20,000 (trade-in)	0.7130	4,260
		Total present value	$199,684
		Initial investment	200,000
		Net present value	($316)

14
LEASING

In the preceding chapter we had a look at various methods of decision making for the purchase of assets like equipment. Another method of obtaining productive assets for a business is to rent or lease.

A lease is a contractual arrangement where the owner of the asset (the lessor) grants you (the lessee) the right to the asset for a specified period of time in return for periodic lease payment. Leasing of land and/or buildings has always been a common method for an entrepreneur to minimize the investment costs of going into business. In recent years, the leasing of equipment and similar items has become more common.

Some suppliers of equipment will lease directly. In other cases, you can lease from a company that specializes in leasing. In other words, the lessor is a company that has bought the equipment from the supplier and has gone into the business of leasing to others. The supplier may act as an intermediary in such cases.

Most equipment leases cannot be canceled and require you to make a series of payments with a sum total that exceeds the cost of assets if purchased outright, since the lessor has to make a profit on his or her investment.

Depreciation of the assets is the lessor's prerogative as owner of the assets. Maintenance is usually, but not invariably, a cost of the lessor.

Generally, the lessor owns any residual value in the assets, although contracts sometimes give you the right to purchase the assets at your option, at a specified price, at the end of the lease period. In such cases the lease purchase is actually a type of conditional sale and you have any tax advantages that claiming expenses such as depreciation may offer.

In some cases you will also have the option to renew the lease for a specified further period.

a. ADVANTAGES OF LEASING EQUIPMENT

As a business operator there may be advantages to you to lease rather than to buy equipment and similar assets.

First, you can avoid the obsolescence and maintenance costs that you might have if the assets are purchased outright. However, the lessor has probably considered the cost of obsolescence (a form of depreciation) and maintenance costs and calculated them into the rental rates. However, a lease contract that allows you to replace obsolete equipment with newer equipment that comes on to the market can give you an advantage over your competitor.

Second, leasing allows you to obtain equipment that you might not be able to afford immediately or could afford only with costly financing. In other words, 100% "financing" of leased assets is possible since there is no down payment required and no loan to be repaid with interest.

Even if you have or can borrow the cash to purchase the assets you need, you may prefer to lease. Leasing allows you to use your available cash for investment in longer life assets, such as land and buildings, that over time frequently appreciate in value, whereas equipment generally depreciates.

Third, since lease payments are generally tax deductible, the lease cost is not as demanding on cash flow as it may at first appear. For example, if you lease an item of equipment for $4,000 a year that is tax deductible and your company is in a 50% tax bracket, the net cash cost of leasing is only $2,000.

	ITEM LEASED	ITEM NOT LEASED
Profit before lease cost	$10,000	$10,000
Lease expense	4,000	0
Profit before tax	$ 6,000	$10,000
Income tax 50%	3,000	5,000
Net profit	$ 3,000	$ 5,000

As you can see by these figures, even though the lease cost is $4,000, the net profit with leasing is only $2,000 less than if the item is not leased.

However, this is an oversimplified situation since, if you owned the asset, you would be able to claim depreciation on it, rather than lease expense, as a tax deduction. Also, if you borrow any money to help finance the purchase of an asset, the interest on that borrowed money is also tax deductible.

Finally, even though with a lease the lessor is generally responsible for maintenance of the equipment while you own it, the lessor also owns any residual value in the asset at the end of the lease period. The lease contract may give you the right to purchase the asset at that time, at a specified price, or you may have the option to renew the lease for a further specified period of time.

Because of these variables, which mean that lease arrangements can vary widely, you would be wise to obtain all necessary financial information prior to making the decision whether to buy or lease any item.

A disadvantage of leasing equipment is that any money borrowed to make the lease payments can be more expensive — by an interest point or more — than money borrowed to purchase the equipment outright.

Also, the lessor is the owner of the equipment and has the right to repossess it if you do not meet the payments. If you owned the equipment, you would not lose any residual value remaining in the equipment.

One of the ways to help you make that decision, once you have all the facts, is to use the concept of discounted cash flow, discussed in chapter 13. This will help you narrow those facts down to a purely financial comparison.

b. A CASE STUDY

Dan's distribution company is considering the purchase of all the vehicles it needs for $250,000. Since the company has a well-established record with its bank, it can borrow the entire $250,000 required. The loan will be repayable in four equal annual installments of principal ($62,500 a year) plus interest at 8%. The vehicles will be depreciated over five years at $50,000 a year, and are assumed to have no trade-in value at the end of that period. The company is in a 50% tax bracket.

As an alternative to purchasing, the company can lease the delivery vehicles at a rental cost of $60,000 a year.

Dan's first step, with the purchase proposal, is to prepare a bank loan repayment schedule showing principal and interest payments for each of the four years of the loan. (See Sample #27.)

SAMPLE #27
BANK LOAN REPAYMENT SCHEDULE

Year	Interest At 8%	Principal	Balance amount
0			$250,000
1	$20,000	$62,500	187,500
2	15,000	62,500	125,000
3	10,000	62,500	62,500
4	5,000	62,500	0

Next, with the purchase plan, the net cash outflow for each of the five years must be calculated, as shown in Sample #28. Since depreciation and the bank loan interest expense are tax deductible, and since the company is in a 50% tax bracket, there is an annual income tax savings equal to 50% of the total of those two expenses.

Thus, in year 1, the expenses of $70,000 are offset by the $35,000 tax savings. The net cost, after tax, is therefore only $35,000. This $35,000 cost has to be increased by the principal repayment on the loan of $62,500, and reduced by the depreciation expense of $50,000 (since depreciation does not require an outlay of cash).

The result is that, in year 1, the net cash outflow is $47,500. Net cash outflow figures are calculated in a similar way for the other four years.

In year 5, since the bank loan has been paid off, there is no interest and bank loan payment to be adjusted for; for this reason the net cash flow is positive (because $25,000 less is paid in income tax) rather than negative.

Sample #29 shows Dan's calculation of the annual net cash outflows under the rental option. Note that, with this option, there is no depreciation expense since the company does not own the vehicles, and no interest or principal payments since no money is to be borrowed.

Finally, Dan transfers the net cash flow figures to Sample #30 and discounts them back using the appropriate discount factor (in Dan's case 8%) from Table #4. Sample #30 shows that from a present value point of view, it would be better to rent in this particular case, since total present value of the cash outflows is lower by $8,903 ($128,681 - $119,778).

Since the decision in Dan's case favors leasing, this does not mean that the decision will always be to lease. The many variables involved can change from situation to situation. For this reason, each case must be judged on its own merits.

For example, in a purchase plan, a company might use some of its own cash as down payment and thus borrow less from the bank. Also, under a purchase plan, there might be a trade-in value of the equipment at the end of its useful life. Further, with a lease, there might be a purchase option to the lessee at the end of the period. If the purchase option is to be exercised the additional cash outflow at the time must be considered. Finally, the terms on borrowed money can change from time to time, and different methods of depreciation can be used. For example, the use of an accelerated depreciation method will give higher depreciation expense in the earlier years, thus reducing income tax and increasing the cash flow in those years.

Because of all these and even other possibilities, each situation must be investigated on its own merits, using all the known variables in the calculations before you make your final decision.

c. LAND AND BUILDING LEASE

One thing you must consider when starting a new business or expanding a successful existing one (unless you have a lot of money to invest) is whether or not to buy land and construct a building or buy land and/or an existing building.

Generally, most first-time business owners invest far too much money in bricks and mortar (the building) when they should be leasing that asset, particularly in the early years. To a lesser degree the same is true of equipment and fixtures.

It is in the early years that the risk is often the greatest, and you may not be able to afford the heavy mortgage debt load that owning land and/or a building and expense equipment obliges. In fact, many leases can be arranged that allow a later purchase option.

However, there may be exceptions. For example, to establish a franchised business the franchisor may insist that you own a freestanding building. In such situations the franchisor ought to be able to provide the financing, or help in finding financing.

SAMPLE #28
ANNUAL NET CASH OUTFLOW WITH PURCHASE

	Year 1	Year 2	Year 3	Year 4	Year 5
Interest expense (from Sample #27)	$20,000	$15,000	$10,000	$ 5,000	0
Depreciation expense	50,000	50,000	50,000	50,000	$50,000
Total tax deductible expense	$70,000	$65,000	$60,000	$55,000	$50,000
Income tax saving 50%	(35,000)	(32,500)	(30,000)	(27,500)	(25,000)
After tax cost	$35,000	$32,500	$30,000	$27,500	$25,000
Add: Principal payments	62,500	62,500	62,500	62,500	0
Deduct: depreciation	(50,000)	(50,000)	(50,000)	(50,000)	(50,000)
Net cash outflow (inflow)	$47,500	$45,000	$42,500	$40,000	($25,000)

SAMPLE #29
ANNUAL NET CASH OUTFLOW WITH RENTAL

	Year 1	Year 2	Year 3	Year 4	Year 5
Rent expense	$60,000	$60,000	$60,000	$60,000	$60,000
Income tax saving 50%	(30,000)	(30,000)	(30,000)	(30,000)	(30,000)
Net cash outflow	$30,000	$30,000	$30,000	$30,000	$30,000

SAMPLE #30
TOTAL PRESENT VALUE OF PURCHASE VS. RENT

	PURCHASE			RENT		
Year	Annual cash outflow (inflow)	Discount factor 8%	Present value	Annual cash outflow	Discount factor 8%	Present value
1	$47,500	0.9259	$43,980	$30,000	0.9259	$ 27,777
2	45,000	0.8573	38,579	30,000	0.8573	25,719
3	42,500	0.7938	33,737	30,000	0.7938	23,814
4	40,000	0.7350	29,400	30,000	0.7350	22,050
5	(25,000)	0.6806	(17,015)	30,000	0.6806	20,418
	Total present value		$128,681		Total present value	$119,778

A lease is basically a partnership agreement between the landlord (the owner of the land and/or building) and the tenant. There is invariably a very direct relationship between the amount of rent charged for business premises and the pedestrian or traffic count — the higher the count the higher the rent.

However, a low rent location can sometimes be overcome by spending more on advertising. But if the amount spent on advertising is greater than the rent saving there is obviously no net benefit in choosing that location.

If your business is such that the customer must find you, you should rent premises that are easy to find and easy to reach.

1. Bare leases

When checking out rentable premises, do more than look at the space and determine how large the square foot area is. See if the walls, floor, and ceiling are finished. If not, find out who pays to put the premises in a rentable condition.

Some premises, even in shopping centers, are rented as bare leases. Premises rented this way are referred to as a "shell." Generally the utilities are brought only to the walls (stubbed in). You pay for all inside finishing including lighting, plumbing, window coverings, and heating and air conditioning equipment. Determine in advance how much this is going to cost so that there are no unhappy surprises.

It is normal that any special inside finishing is your responsibility. However, if you are going to do any extensive internal remodeling that would subsequently benefit the landlord when your lease expires, see if you can negotiate a reduced rent.

2. Lease agreements

There is no standard form of lease agreement. Each lease agreement must be prepared by the lawyers of the two parties involved depending on the particular circumstances of the situation.

The agreement should cover matters such as the length of the contract (for example, 5, 10, or even 20 or more years), the amount of rent and frequency of payment, the responsibility of the 2 parties for the maintenance of the property, and who pays which costs for major items, such as plumbing, electrical, air conditioning, or minor items, such as cleaning and cleaning supplies. Other items of cost such as building alterations, property taxes, and insurance should also be in the agreement.

3. Expense pass-throughs

Some lease contracts contain expense pass-throughs. In other words some of the landlord's "normal" expenses become the responsibility of the tenant.

The most common pass-through is known as a triple net lease in which the tenant pays for all maintenance, property taxes, and building insurance. This can have a double effect. Any remodeling you do (such as building improvements) increases the value of the building and will thus increase your property taxes, even though you don't own the building.

Similarly, businesses in the area may be assessed a special property tax for improved community lighting, sewers, or other works. As a tenant under triple net you will pay that added burden.

Read the contract carefully, and have your lawyer go over it since some leases state that if you attach anything to the floors, walls, or ceilings it becomes the property of the lessor. This means that you could invest several thousand dollars in shelving, special lighting, equipment fixed to the floor, and so on, and as soon as you install it, it is no longer legally yours.

4. Restrictions

Check the contract carefully to see if there are any landlord imposed restrictions on your business operations, such as restrictions on subletting, which you may want to do if the business is not successful and your lease still has some time to run.

The landlord should not have the right to unreasonably withhold your right to sublet, assign, or mortgage your lease, or even sell it for its remaining life, including options (see next section) to someone else. If your business is successful, the right to sell its goodwill for a profit can be quite valuable to you.

Measure your floor space so that if rent is based on square foot area, you will not be charged for more space than you have. However, note that in some shopping malls "your" space includes a share of common areas such as halls, storage areas, and elevators. Find out in advance what your share of this common space is.

5. Renewal option

An initial relatively short contract with one or more renewal options is often preferable to a long-term lease contract. Renewal options prevent you from being locked in if the business is not successful, but allow you to continue if it is a profitable enterprise. Any renewal options and their terms should be written into the initial contract.

In some older buildings in a city core, landlords may be reluctant to include options since they never know when an offer may come along from an investor wishing to tear down the building and construct a new one. Your successful business with two or three renewals could be in the way of the landlord.

6. Fixtures and equipment

The typical lease is generally only for the land and building, with the lessee (operator) purchasing and owning the fixtures and equipment. If the equipment and similar items are owned by the lessor (in which case the lease payments will generally be higher), the lease agreement should specify how frequently these items are to be replaced and at whose cost.

If you own the equipment and similar items, the lease contract should provide for the disposition of them at the end of the lease period.

The two most common arrangements are that you are responsible for complete removal of such items at your cost, or that the lessor has the right to buy them at some stipulated value.

7. Contingencies

Make sure any necessary contingencies are in the contract. Contingencies might be that the contract is dependent on your obtaining necessary financing for equipment purchases or that all necessary government licenses, permits, and variances are approved. Finally, a contingency that you may inspect the site to see that it conforms to the lease description should be included.

d. RENTAL ARRANGEMENT

With any form of lease operation, it is normal for you to bear the burden of any operating losses, although, depending on the lease arrangement, some of the net profit may have to be shared with the lessor under certain circumstances.

There are a variety of rental arrangement possibilities with leasing. Some of these are fixed rental, variable rental, percentage of sales, and percentage of profit.

1. Fixed rental

A fixed rental arrangement calls for straight payments during the term of the lease. The payment might be a stepped one that increases, for example, year by year during the term of the lease. However, the payments are not variable with, and do not depend on, your sales or profits.

The lease agreement will probably allow renegotiation of the fixed amount of rent during the life of the agreement, particularly if the life is for an extended number of years.

2. Variable rental

A variable rental has a fixed portion, usually at least sufficient to give the landlord cash flow to amortize loan obligations, cover expenses, and provide a return on investment. In addition, there will be additional rent based either on your gross sales or on your net profit.

The variable rent portion gives the landlord some hedge against inflation, although there might be a ceiling rent amount stated in the contract.

3. Percentage of sales

Another possibility is for rent to be based on sales. If so, what is to be included in sales should be completely spelled out. For example, is rental income from a cigarette vending machine located in your business's reception area to be included in sales?

Most contracts allow for a declining percentage as sales increase. For example, rent may be 6% of sales up to a certain level, then decline to 5% for any sales above that level.

Some contracts call for an increasing percentage of sales as sales increase — an escalation clause. This can be risky for you since the accelerating percentage can seriously erode normal net profit margins as sales continue to climb.

4. Percentage of profit

When rent is partly based on percentage of sales, the landlord is in a type of partnership arrangement with you. With the variable portion of rent based on profit, this partnership becomes even more firm. The profit must be carefully defined in the least contract as either profit before income tax, profit before interest and tax, or profit before depreciation, interest, and tax.

In some lease contracts, to protect the landlord, the amount of certain types of expenses may be limited. For example, if your salary is not limited, you could pay yourself such an inflated amount that there would be no profit to be shared with the landlord by way of rent.

In other cases the contract may specify a minimum expense amount that you must spend each year, for example, for advertising so that sufficient sales and profit are generated or for maintenance so that the building is kept in good condition.

e. SALE/LEASEBACK

One other type of arrangement is the sale/leaseback. A sale/leaseback arrangement can be very useful for increasing a company's cash flow. Under a sale/leaseback, an owner of a building sells the property to an investor under an agreement to lease it back for business purposes. Alternatively, the business person may own or rent the land, put up a building, and then sell both land (if owned) and building under an agreement to lease them back.

The sale/leaseback is useful for a small, growing company that does not have ready access to credit on favorable terms for expansion. But, even larger companies use the sale/leaseback as a method of freeing up capital in land and/or buildings when that capital can be more effectively used to increase the return on investment via expansion, upgrading, or some other method.

Sale/leaseback can also be useful for a well-established company that has owned its own building for so long that its depreciation base is now low. Selling the building may produce more than sufficient cash to compensate for recaptured depreciation and capital gain on the sale and also provide an ongoing rental expense that will help minimize the income tax burden.

Under some sale/leaseback arrangements, you may also be able to structure the contract so that, at the end of the lease period, you regain ownership of the building and/or the land.

Sale/leaseback is not the answer to all leasing problems, but it can have advantages. Just remember to evaluate each case individually to determine what is best for you.

f. ADVANTAGES OF LEASING

Some advantages of leasing are the following:

(a) Under a lease arrangement you have the obvious advantage of not having to provide capital to buy the property. Any capital you might have is then available for investment elsewhere.

(b) Your borrowing power is freed up to raise money, if required, for more critical areas of the business.

(c) Lease payments on a building are generally fully tax deductible.

(d) Owned land is not depreciable for tax purposes, but the cost of leasing land is tax deductible.

(e) Any leasehold improvements that you make to the building are generally amortized over the life of the lease rather than over the life of the building. The lease period is normally less than the building life therefore providing a tax saving.

(f) You may have a purchase option at the end of the lease period when it may be desirable to buy the land and/or building and cash is available to do this.

(g) If and when the time comes to sell the business, it may be easier to do if there is no real estate involved.

(h) Although you would not normally have this in mind when entering a lease transaction, in case of unexpected bankruptcy, you would probably only be liable for one year's rent rather than long-term mortgage payments on a property you purchased.

(i) Finally, it may be possible to arrange a lease with rental payments adjusted to the business's seasonal cash flows, even though total annual rent would be the same amount.

g. DISADVANTAGES OF LEASING

Some disadvantages of leasing are these:

(a) Any capital gain in the assets accrues to the landlord and not to you. In a similar way, at the expiry of the lease, the value of the future profit of the business that you have worked hard to build up does not benefit you unless the lease is renewed.

(b) The cost of a lease may be higher than some other form of financing.

(c) It may also be more difficult for you to borrow money with leased premises if there are no assets (other than a lease agreement) to pledge as collateral.

(d) Finally, the total cash outflow in rental payments may be greater in the long run than for purchasing the property.

h. RENTAL AGENTS

If you are negotiating a lease through a rental agent, remember that the agent has only one mandate: to rent empty space for the landlord as quickly as possible to earn a commission.

You should know more about what you want for your particular business than the agent. In other words, be prepared by arming yourself in advance with as many facts as possible about the type and particularly the size of premises you need. Also, be alert to agents whose main motivation is to rent you less than adequate premises, particularly in a poor location for your type of business.

15
EQUITY FINANCING

Regardless of its size, every business needs some form of financing. In general, there are two main sources of financing: debt and equity.

With debt the lender does not have any equity or ownership in the business and, therefore, normally no active say in the day-to-day operations of the business. Banks are one type of debt lender. Their return on the investment (loan) is the interest your business pays for the use of that money. The equity owners' return on their investment is usually in the form of withdrawals (proprietorship or partnerships) or dividends (limited company).

Before you can raise any debt financing you will normally have to show potential lenders that you are willing to invest (and risk) money in the business yourself. If you are not willing to invest in the business yourself, why should an outside lender?

a. EQUITY INVESTORS

Those who generally have an active say in the day-to-day operations of the business are the equity investors — or the owners of the company. This equity investment could range from 10% to 50% of the total investment required. The closer to 50% it is, the easier it will be to borrow and the higher your profits might be (since you will have less interest expense on borrowed money that will eat into those profits).

However, the higher the equity, the lower might be your actual return on investment since you are reducing the

149

opportunity to trade on the lender's investment. This is known as using leverage (see chapter 6).

1. Personal funds

The most common source of equity capital is personal funds from savings. Over the past few years, many entrepreneurs have been able to provide this initial equity because of inflation. Inflation has caused home values to increase to the point that they could be remortgaged to provide a form of instant cash.

2. Friends or relatives

The equity investment could be further increased from the savings of friends willing to invest in shares or loans or even from relatives (love money). However, many otherwise successful small businesses have created problems by bringing in friends and/or relatives as equity investors. Mixing social or family relationships with business is always risky, particularly if the business is not doing as well as everyone initially imagined, or if the terms and conditions of such loans are not clearly spelled out to prevent these lenders insisting on becoming involved in day-to-day matters. Also, if a relative dies, the heirs may immediately demand their money back, with interest, under the threat of a lawsuit.

To avoid these problems, make sure any friend or family loans are covered by written agreements, preferably drawn up by a lawyer. In this way agreements will at least be viewed by those lenders on a businesslike basis. Agreement should be reached on such matters as —

(a) Rate of interest to be paid

(b) When the loans will be retired (paid back), and any option to pay them back early

(c) The procedures that all parties will follow if loans become delinquent

3. Employees

Your employees can be another source of internal equity financing. Employees who have savings may be interested in investing in your company since they understand its products and know and trust its owners. They also feel they are in an advantageous position to closely monitor their investment.

An employee with an investment in a company is also likely to feel more motivated and be concerned about the company's success. The main disadvantage is that it may be difficult to fire or retire an unproductive or uncooperative employee who has an equity investment in your business.

4. Loans versus shares

If your business is incorporated, the equity investment could be in the form of stockholders loans, or common stock or shares (to be discussed in the next section), or a combination of loans and shares if it is an incorporated company. How the owners' or equity investors' investment in the company is structured will vary in each different situation.

However, generally speaking, the advantage of money invested as loans is that it can easily be paid back to lenders without tax, other than personal tax on any interest the lender receives from the company before all the loan is finally paid off.

If the money is in the form of shares, the lenders will find it may be more difficult to get their money back since shares must be sold to someone else or back to the company.

On the other hand, banks and other debt investors are skeptical of equity investor loans because of the ease with which they can be repaid and because it would be feasible to the business to borrow money from a debt lender and use the cash to pay back equity investor loans.

The outside debt investors may, therefore, place restrictions or conditions on when and how the company can pay off shareholder loans, redeem shares, or possibly even pay dividends on shares. These restrictions or conditions are imposed to protect the debt investors.

You should seek the advice of a tax accountant since your personal tax situation and that of other equity investors and the degree of financial success of the business can have a bearing on whether the shareholders' investment should be in the form of loans or shares.

b. SHARES

Unless your company is a proprietorship or partnership, it will have issued some shares. In a one-person company those shares will be held by the owner. A larger company may possibly have several owners or shareholders.

A small company can often raise more equity capital by issuing more shares, for cash, to all its present shareholders who operate the company. It can make financial decisions with little or no formality.

As a business grows larger and operating procedures become more formal, shares may be issued to new shareholders. Major financial decisions must be discussed and approved by the board of directors whose responsibility it is to run the company.

1. Common shares

In most cases the shareholders of smaller companies will own common shares with each share entitling its owner to one vote at shareholder meetings. In closely held companies, where the original owner or owners want to retain full voting power, the voting rights might be limited to a particular class of common shares, and all or most of those shares will be held by the few who wish to retain complete control of, and be responsible for, the company's operations.

Alternatively, different classes of common shares may have equal voting rights, but the quantities issued and the selling prices of each class are arranged so that effective control is still in the hands of those who wish to control the business.

For example, consider the situation of a new company that issues both class A and class B common shares to raise $100,000 of equity capital. Each share of either class carries one vote. Class A shares will be sold for $1 and 80,000 will be issued — total $80,000. Class B shares will be sold for 10¢ and 200,000 will be issued — total $20,000. Thus the B shareholders have effective voting control since they own 2½ times as many shares (200,000 versus 80,000) and yet have put up only 20% of the total equity capital.

Of course, in order to sell the class A shares in this particular way, the class B shareholders generally have to give up something, such as agreeing to receive a lower dividend rate, or no dividends until retained earnings have reached a minimum stipulated level.

The class B shareholders might be quite happy to give up something since they control matters such as future methods of financing, whether or not any dividends will be paid, the form that further common share issues will take including selling prices and voting rights, and similar matters.

2. Advantages of common shares

The major advantage of common share financing is that the shareholders control the company and benefit the most if the company is successful.

Also, with common shares the company is not committed to paying dividends although you would normally expect dividends to be paid if the business is successful.

If the business is successful, the value of its common shares increases and its ability to obtain short, intermediate, and long-term financing (with its advantage of leverage) increases.

In times of inflation the ownership of common shares provides protection even if only against inflation because the assets (such as land and building) usually increase in value. There is also the potential for capital gain on the sale of the shares if the company is taken over by another.

Other advantages of common share financing are that it —

(a) is an easier and faster way to raise money,

(b) expands the borrowing power of the business,

(c) reduces the risk to each of the business's shareholders,

(d) improves the credit rating with suppliers, and

(e) adds the experience and advice of new shareholders to the company.

3. Disadvantages of common shares

The major disadvantage of common share financing is that since common shares are equity and represent ownership of the company, but only after all other liabilities are paid off, common shareholders are the first to suffer if the company is unsuccessful.

Another disadvantage of common shares, particularly to the original investors, is that voting control may be diluted as more shares are issued and more shareholders are involved, although this can be overcome, as illustrated earlier, using nonvoting classes of common shares. Also, dividends to common shareholders are not tax deductible to the company as is interest on debt financing.

Other disadvantages are that —

(a) it may reduce the flexibility of the company since there are more shareholders to contend with, and

(b) it increases costs to the company from issuing additional shares, making dividend payments, and increasing accounting controls and legal and accounting costs, as well as brokerage costs if the company is a public one.

c. PREFERRED SHARES

Common shares are not the only method of equity financing for an incorporated company. Preferred shares can also be issued. Preferred shares usually have priority, with reference to dividends and assets, over common shares. Dividend priority is usually limited to a dividend rate stated as a fixed percentage of the par, or face, value of the preferred shares.

However, to the company, payment of dividends is not a legal obligation as is the payment of interest on a mortgage. In other words, the company will only pay dividends on preferred shares if it has the money to do so.

1. Cumulative preferred

To protect the preferred shareholders in such situations, preferred shares are usually cumulative. This means if the dividend is not paid, it accumulates and must eventually be paid before any dividends can be paid to the holders of common shares.

2. Classes of preferred

Various classes of preferred shares can also be issued carrying different voting rights. These voting rights can be full (on an equal basis, share for share, with common stock), nonvoting, or limited voting. With limited voting preferred shareholders might obtain full voting rights if the company does not pay its preferred share dividends.

3. Redeemable preferred

Redeemable preferred shares may be issued. The redeemable feature allows your company the option to buy back those preferred shares at a stipulated price usually at or above the preferred shares' face or par value. By issuing redeemable preferred shares, a company, when it has the cash, can cancel inhibiting, restrictive covenants (see below) that the preferred shares placed on common stock owners.

4.   Convertible preferred

As an alternative to redeemable preferred stock, shares may be made convertible at the preferred shareholders' choice. In other words, the preferred shareholder, when the time is right, has the option to convert the preferred into a stipulated number of common shares.

5.   Advantages of preferred

Since preferred shares are a form of equity financing, the selling of preferred shares to raise money broadens the equity base and could make future debt financing easier since it reduces the debt to equity ratio.

Also, even though preferred shares may carry a stipulated dividend rate that may also be cumulative, those dividends, unlike interest on a mortgage, do not have to be paid on a specified date if the company is currently short of cash.

Finally, issuing preferred shares is a method of using equity financing without losing or diluting voting control as long as dividends can be paid.

6.   Disadvantages of preferred

A major disadvantage of preferred share financing is that dividends are not deductible by the company for income tax purposes. Consider the situation of a company that requires $100,000 for expansion and expects to earn, before interest and income taxes, $18,000 on this additional investment. The company is in a 50% tax bracket and can obtain the $100,000 either by a 15% loan or by issuing 15% preferred shares. The following shows the net profit remaining for common shareholders under either alternative. In this situation, preferred shares are a disadvantage.

156

	Loan financing	Preferred share financing
Income before interest and tax	$18,000	$18,000
Interest 15% x $100,000	15,000	
Profit before income tax	$ 3,000	$18,000
Income tax 50%	1,500	9,000
Profit before dividends	$ 1,500	$ 9,000
Preferred share dividends		15,000
Net profit (loss)	$ 1,500	($ 6,000)

However, despite the above, financial decisions must also consider the effect of a proposed financing arrangement on potential investors. It may be easier to raise money from preferred shares than from a loan. Investors may be attracted to the preferred shares because of a participating dividend or from being able to sell back their preferred shares to the company at a profit, or by being able to eventually convert them into common shares.

7. Restrictions

Preferred stock may restrict the actions of common shareholders. For example, this can be done by restricting the issuing of further preferred shares ranking equally or ahead of issued preferred without those shareholders' approval.

There may be other restrictions such as the amount or type of further debt that may be assumed, or a limit on the payment of dividends on common shares, to profits generated subsequent to the issuing of the preferred shares and then only if working capital is above a certain specified amount.

d. DIVIDEND POLICY

A dividend policy is necessary for any company that has shareholders. This policy is necessary so that the company's profits can be effectively divided between reinvestment in the company for its continued growth or expansion, or payment of dividends to the shareholders.

Shareholders expect dividends (since that is often the reason they purchased shares in the first place), but if the company's objective is growth this may necessitate the retention of some, if not all, of the profits or retained earnings of the business. In such a case the objectives of company growth and dividend payments are in conflict and the company's dividend policy is therefore a critical financial decision in all but one-person companies.

Dividends can only be paid from current or previous years' retained earnings. Further, in order to protect the creditors, the law prohibits a company paying dividends if liabilities exceed assets (in other words, if the company is insolvent).

Even if assets exceed liabilities, a company must have cash available to pay dividends and, as you know from chapter 12, a profit does not necessarily mean that cash is available.

Sometimes dividend restrictions are imposed by lenders. For example, a bank debt lender may require that a minimum working capital level must be maintained before dividends that would impair working capital can be paid. Also, if preferred shares have been issued, dividends usually have to be paid on those preferred shares before common stock dividends can be paid.

A company that is expanding rapidly will generally use most of its accumulated profits for expansion, leaving less for dividends. A company with relatively stable and predictable earnings will usually pay out more of its earnings, on a percentage basis, than a company whose earnings are cyclical or difficult to predict.

e. GOING PUBLIC

Small and closely held companies do not face the dilemma of whether or not to go public. However, as a company grows, even without wide common share ownership, it can end up going public as a result of shareholders selling off their shares to "outsiders."

However, the procedure of going public formally in order to sell the shares widely requires the company to conform to the laws concerning the sale of securities. Any company wishing to go public must follow the required procedures.

If a company's shares are traded through brokers, but not through an organized stock exchange, it is referred to as "over the counter." Once a company has grown sufficiently, particularly in number of shareholders and public acceptance and marketability of its shares, you may wish to consider a formal listing with a stock exchange, although such a listing by itself does not guarantee an active trading of the shares.

1. Disadvantages

There are more disadvantages to an exchange listing. For example, more public attention is focused on companies that are listed. Also, if the value of the company's shares declines in difficult times, speculators may be attracted and a takeover or merger may become possible and control lost by the original company developers. The likelihood of speculative manipulation of the shares may also be increased causing wide pricing fluctuations.

Finally, when shares are publicly traded, management frequently becomes concerned with what is happening to the price of the shares rather than making sound, long-run business decisions.

The decision to go public is a serious one. Raising funds through a new issue of shares to the public is a long, arduous, and precarious process requiring good timing. It can take from three to six months and cost anywhere from $25,000 to $100,000. It should, therefore, not even be contemplated unless you require a very large amount of money — say, at least $500,000.

In order to arrange a sale of shares to the public, you will need an investment dealer or financial negotiator with the expertise to bring together a company that requires capital with those who have money to invest.

2. Selling shares to a larger company

One other possibility is to sell shares to a larger company. Larger companies are sometimes interested in investing in smaller companies without taking control. Their motivation is the desire to become involved with an individual or small company in an unfamiliar business field with the intention of expanding into it in a major way at some later date.

Alternatively, the operations of the large and small companies may be complementary to each other.

In any such situation you would be well advised to seek the help of your accountant, lawyer, and other professional advisors very early in the discussions.

16
DEBT FINANCING

In this chapter, we take a look at two matters related to debt financing: interest rates and security. In the following chapters we cover the various types of debt financing available and the sources of financing.

a. INTEREST

Banks and other financial institutions vary interest rates according to money market conditions. The rates can change frequently.

Lending institutions use money from various sources to make their loans. The amount of interest that the lender is paying to use those funds and the length of the loan determine the interest that the lender will charge you.

Rates also vary depending on the customer. The prime rate is generally the lowest rate available. Rates increase above that depending on the specific business, its credit rating, its size, and other factors. It would not be unreasonable (because of the risk involved to the lender) to suggest that most small businesses in need of bank credit pay rates are among the highest.

1. Short-term loans

Interest on short-term loans reflects the interest rate currently paid by the lender on short-term deposits such as savings accounts. The interest paid on savings accounts depends on money market conditions or the supply and demand for short-term funds. International borders are not necessarily ignored in the equation since those with funds to deposit in banks will often seek out the most favorable rates, regardless of country.

The best indicator of short-term interest rates of various kinds is the prime rate — the lowest rate that an individual lender charges to its largest and most credit-worthy customers.

Small businesses are usually not large enough to be considered candidates for the prime rate, but by keeping an eye on the daily quote fluctuations in the prime rate, the small business borrower can have a good idea how much above the prime rate must be paid to obtain short-term funds.

2. Long-term loans

Lenders who have pools of funds available from depositors who have left money with them for a minimum of at least a year, and preferably longer, may be able to lend money for longer terms and at lower rates than those charged on short-term loans. However, in volatile money markets where interest rates are unpredictable, long-term lending rates can be higher than current short-term rates since they are sometimes fixed and not subject to change during the term of the loan.

Because of this situation, and because lenders have been hurt in volatile money markets, you may be unable to find a fixed interest rate on a long-term loan.

These long-term loans are subject to two or three-year terms and balloon payments. A balloon payment means that at the end of the term the balance of the loan is technically due and payable. However, in practice the lender can renegotiate the loan (generally in the lender's favor) at that time, adjusting the interest rate and other terms.

Variable rate long-term loans are also becoming more common. A variable rate long-term loan simply means that the interest rates are adjustable, at the discretion of the lender, as frequently as monthly. The rate may go up or down depending on money market conditions. These

162

market conditions take into consideration the current inflation rate and the market's expectation of the future inflation rate.

3. Interest spread

Borrowers frequently ask why the rate paid on savings accounts or other bank deposits is less, sometimes as much as three or four points, than the amount charged on loans.

The reason is that the bank has its expenses, just as your business has, for operating costs (such as interest paid on deposits, rent, wages, supplies) and overhead expenses (such as management salaries, building rent, insurance) and must itself have a difference between the total of those costs and the income it receives in interest and service charges received. In other words, the lender must make a profit and a reasonable return on investment.

In addition, just as you may make sales to individuals or companies who are unable to pay their accounts, so too the lender must "absorb" losses on loans made to individuals or companies who are unable to pay.

These losses are not in fact absorbed by the lender any more than the losses you sustain in your business are absorbed by you. They are built into the selling price you charge for goods and services, and a money lender builds them into the selling price — that is, the interest rate charged.

However, since bankers, just like you, are in competition with other lenders or other businesses, their interest rates are competitive, just as your prices have to be. This means that you should search out the lender with the most favorable lending rate and conditions just as you would expect astute customers to seek you out if you offered the best quality at a competitive price.

Generally, however you will find that the larger the amount you wish to borrow, the longer the period of the loan, and the greater the risk the lender considers it to be, the higher the interest rate. The more stable the company, the longer it has been in business, the larger it is, and similar factors tend to reduce the risk and, therefore, the interest rate to the borrower.

b. SECURITY

Most lenders require some sort of security for loans made to small businesses. For intermediate- and long-term loans this security is quite specific and is discussed in chapter 18. For short-term loans of a year or less this security will probably take the form of one or more of the following:

(a) Personal guarantees

(b) Assignment of lease

(c) Warehouse receipt

(d) Savings accounts

(e) Life insurance

(f) Stocks and bonds

1. Personal guarantees

Even if your business is incorporated, the lender may require your personal guarantee or endorsement of the loan in the event your company does not meet its debt obligations. This means that if your company defaults on its repayments, the lender can claim against your personal assets such as your savings, your home, and your car.

If your case for a loan is not a strong one, you will normally have little choice but to provide this personal guarantee or endorsement. If there are other partners or shareholders in the company, they might also be required to sign guarantees.

In some cases, where neither you nor other principals in the company can provide sufficient security to the lender, you may be asked to find an outside guarantor. If your case is so weak that you need an outside guarantor, you might question whether or not you should really be making the loan in the first place.

A guarantee may be limited or unlimited. A limited guarantee gives the lender the right to demand that you repay, on request, the amount owing on that specific loan. An unlimited guarantee gives the lender the right to demand that you repay, on request, all loans due to that lender. Obviously it is preferable for you to have a limited guarantee.

Make sure that when any guaranteed loan is paid off you obtain a release from the guarantee. If a personal guarantee is required by the lender in addition to other security, try to negotiate a guarantee only for the amount of the shortfall and not for the full amount of the loan.

Also, if you have made your own direct loan to your company and were obliged by the debt lender to sign a postponement of claim for it, make sure that the postponement is canceled after the debt lender is paid off.

Similarly, if restrictions were placed on payment of dividends to you during the period of the debt, or if life insurance policies were assigned to the lender, have these restrictions removed and/or the policies changed to revert to you.

It may be that your company has made loans to you or other principals in the company. If so the lender may require you and the others to subordinate your claims to those of the lender by signing an appropriate subordination agreement.

2. Assignment of lease

You may be in the business of leasing out assets in which case the security for the lender may be an assigned lease or leases. An assigned lease is similar to a guarantee. The bank or other institution lends the money on the security of a leased asset and is assigned the lease and the lender (instead of you) automatically receives the rent payments which go toward reducing the loan.

3. Warehouse receipt

Lenders sometimes require a warehouse receipt as security for a loan. This receipt is delivered to the lender and shows that the commodity or product used as security is either in a public warehouse or on your premises. The warehouse receipt is for a percentage of the estimated value of the items used as security, and these items normally have to be readily marketable.

4. Savings accounts

You may be able to obtain a loan, all else failing, by assigning your personal savings account to the lender as security. While it is assigned your withdrawals from it will be limited.

5. Life insurance

Instead of raising cash from your insurance company based on your policy's paid up cash value, you may be able to assign your policy instead to a bank, which may be an easier and speedier method of obtaining the cash.

6. Stocks and bonds

If you have marketable stocks and bonds, you may be able to use them as security or collateral for a loan. These have to be gilt-edged stocks, and the maximum you can expect might be up to 75% of their market value.

Alternatively, if you have government bonds, it might go as high as 90%. If the market value on your stocks and/or bonds drops while they are secured, you may have to put up additional security or reduce the loan.

17
SHORT-TERM FINANCING

Short-term financing is generally considered to be funding required for a period of less than a year. In short-term financing, the lender will tend to place greater emphasis on your balance sheet in order to see if, in case of your business's liquidation, current assets would provide sufficient funds to repay the debt. This differs from intermediate- and long-term financing (discussed in the next chapter) where lenders rely more on the earnings of your company and its ability to repay longer loans out of ongoing profits.

One basic rule of finance is that short-term requirements for cash should be provided by short-term financing, and longer-term requirements by intermediate- or long-term financing.

If this rule is not followed, you might end up with a financing imbalance. For example, if you made a short-term one-year bank loan and used the money to buy long-life equipment, you might find yourself short of cash to purchase inventory, carry receivables, pay your payables, or even pay back the one-year loan! You could even be forced into liquidation or bankruptcy in such a situation.

a. INTERNAL FINANCING

One method of raising short-term funding is by internal financing, which is sometimes referred to as bootstrap financing. This means using your company's ability to generate cash or capital from profits, thus reducing the need for equity and debt financing.

Earlier, some of the ways to generate internal cash through effective working capital management were discussed. When you can indicate to a lender that you are practicing good working capital management and maximizing the use of internal funds, you will be more likely to find external short-term financing on reasonable terms when you need it.

b. TRADE CREDIT

Surprisingly the most common means of short-term financing is trade credit or financial assistance from companies you buy from. The reason for this is that most suppliers do not demand cash on delivery (COD) other than in those cases where a business has a reputation for delinquency in payment of accounts.

Usually a bill or invoice for purchases is sent at the month end. In the case of, let us say, a 30-day payment period for items purchased at the beginning of a month this would mean that you use the service or supplies received without cost for anywhere up to 60 days.

To a small business this type of trade credit is an important source of cash. Even if you had the cash to pay the bill at the time it was received it may not be wise to do so.

As long as there is no penalty imposed you are free to let your cash sit in the bank and collect interest until the invoice has to be paid. To you this is another source of profit.

1. Open credit

This type of trade credit is sometimes called "open credit" since it is generally arranged on an understanding between buyer and seller without any formal agreement in writing.

One type of open credit arrangement is for the supplier to extend credit for a specific number of days after delivery of the goods, or after the month end following delivery of the goods, with no cash discount permitted. In other words, the full amount of the invoice or invoices must be paid.

Another arrangement is for the supplier to offer both a credit period and a cash discount. One common discount type is referred to as 2/10, net 30. This means that you are offered a 2% discount off the invoice price if the bill is paid within 10 days. If the bill is not paid within the 10-day period, it must be paid within a further 20 days but without discount. This type of arrangement is made to encourage you to pay bills promptly (purchase discounts were discussed in chapter 12).

Another type of trade credit is to obtain goods on consignment. When you receive goods on consignment the supplier retains ownership of them. You only pay the supplier when the goods are sold.

2. Establishing credit

If your business is relatively new and on COD with suppliers, you may initially have to borrow to pay those suppliers in order to establish and maintain good relations and build up a solid credit base. You should also be ready to provide a supplier with prompt credit references to help establish your trade credit. Most larger suppliers will have credit departments, or will employ a credit agency, to check on your credit status if you are a new customer.

When you have established a good credit standing with a supplier you should pay your bills on time, otherwise you might find yourself being reverted to a COD basis. Maintaining a good credit record with a supplier may mean that one day your supplier might be interested in investing money in your business if you are expanding.

As you build up your credit record with suppliers, you might later be able to negotiate more favorable trade credit terms, such as extending the time period before payment is required or receiving a larger discount on invoices paid promptly.

However, don't become too attached to one or two suppliers simply because they provide liberal trade credit terms.

You might find you are locked into a situation where a supplier no longer remain competitive in price, quality, delivery, or service.

In the discussion so far it is assumed that you pay bills by the end of the supplier's payment period. If you delay paying beyond that date, you are using this "free" money at a further cost to the supplier. Banks and other lending institutions also look unfavorably on businesses that make a habit of not paying bills promptly.

If you have this reputation, you might well find that suppliers will deliver only on a COD basis. You might also find it difficult to borrow funds when needed for short-term purposes.

3. Special situations

If the nature of your business is seasonal, you might find it difficult to pay all bills in the off season when they are due. In such cases it might be wise to arrange for a longer payment period with suppliers whose financial resources allow them to extend longer credit. Alternatively, arrangements could be made with a lending institution to borrow funds for the interim period so that bills can be paid within the normal payment period.

Keep suppliers, particularly major ones, advised if you are going to have to defer payment of their account for some reason. Alerting suppliers this way might prevent ill will and credit curtailment if, for example, your business is suffering a slight downturn in difficult economic times.

Don't forget that in difficult economic conditions the supplier might also be forced into curtailing trade credit. In other words, trade credit is not a right that you have in perpetuity.

Finally you should also recognize that trade credit is not absolutely free. The supplier who extends credit also has financing costs, which must be paid out of revenue from the products sold. In other words, the cost is included in the selling prices. Where competition exists among suppliers, however, this hidden cost should be minimized.

c. SHORT-TERM OR OPERATING LOANS

Short-term or operating loans (sometimes referred to as commercial loans) are for financing inventory, accounts receivable, special purchases, prepaid promotions, and other items requiring working capital during peak periods. Normally up to 10% of annual sales can be borrowed to finance such requirements.

These loans are considered to be self-liquidating since they are paid back when the inventory or receivables financed by them are converted to cash that is then used to pay off the loan.

The main sources of short-term loans are commercial banks or similar financing institutions. Using a short-term loan is a good way to establish credit with a bank. When such a lender considers a short-term loan it will be very interested in your business's liquidity. If you have a healthy working capital, collect your accounts receivable promptly and have a rapid rate of inventory turnover, your business will be a good prospect for a short-term loan.

1. Security required

This type of loan could be secured or unsecured. If secured, the security might be any or all of the following:

(a) A fixed or floating charge debenture on accounts receivable, inventory, equipment, or fixtures. The lender can register this debenture in a similar way to a mortgage on land and building.

(b) A general assignment of your accounts receivable. You collect the receivables in the normal way unless you are in default of the loan. In that case the lender assumes collection of the receivables. When

171

receivables are assigned, you normally have to submit to the lender a list of the outstanding ones each month.

(c) An assignment of fire insurance and, in some cases, key employee or personal life insurance policies

(d) Stocks and bonds that you or your company owns

(e) A personal guarantee by you and/or your spouse (when personal assets are registered in the spouse's name)

2. Terms

Short-term loans are usually negotiated for specific periods of time (e.g., 30, 60, or 90 days and less frequently for periods up to a year or more) and may be repayable in a lump sum at the end of the period or in periodic installments. If you have adequate collateral, short-term loans of up to a year can sometimes be negotiated.

Each separate borrowing is usually covered by a promissory note (a form of contract spelling out the interest rate and terms of the loan), and the interest rate is frequently subject to change, particularly in erratic money markets.

3. Interest rate

The interest rate is usually a stated annual rate. The stated rate may differ from the effective (or true) rate if the loan is discounted. Discounting means that the interest on the loan is deducted in advance.

If a $1,000 bank loan is taken out at the beginning of the year, to be prepaid at the end of the year at a discount (interest) rate of 15%, you would receive $850 ($1,000, less 15% of $1,000, or $150), and repay $1,000 at the end of the year. Since you have only $850, the effective interest rate is —

$$\frac{\$150}{\$850} \times 100 = 17.6\%$$

The effective interest rate also differs from the stated rate if a loan is repayable in equal installments over the term of the loan, rather than in a lump sum at the end of the loan period as in the case above.

Consider a $1,200 loan at a 12% rate, repayable in equal monthly installments of principal over a year ($100 per month) plus interest. If the interest is calculated on the initial loan, it will be 12% of $1,200, or $144 ($12 per month). The effective rate of interest will be higher than the stated 12% since you do not have the use of the full $1,200 for the year.

Tables are available from most bookstores or stationery retailers from which an exact rate of interest can be determined under various circumstances, but an approximate effective rate of interest can be quickly calculated.

With equal monthly repayments, on average the borrower has only half the $1,200 for use over the year, or $600 ($1,200 divided by 2). The effective interest rate is then —

$$\frac{\$144}{\$600} \times 100 = 24\%$$

which is double the stated rate.

In all cases where money is being borrowed, and particularly where you are shopping around for the best rate, it is important to know what the effective interest rate is.

d. LINE OF CREDIT

A line of credit is an agreement between you and a bank, or similar financial institution, specifying the maximum amount of credit (overdraft) the bank will allow you at any one time. Credit lines are usually established for one-year periods, subject to annual renegotiation and renewal, with the bank taking your accounts receivable and inventory as security.

Generally, accounts receivable, as long as they are not overdue, may be financed up to 75% and inventory up to 50%.

A line of credit is useful for a seasonal business with a need to carry considerably more inventory and at the same time carry a much larger than normal accounts receivable from charge sales that create a peak season financial need.

The amount of credit is based on the bank's assessment of the creditworthiness of the company and its credit requirements. This type of loan is sometimes called a demand loan since the bank can demand that it be repaid immediately without notice. However, this would not happen under normal circumstances.

If you are a borrower whose company has a record of profitability, you may qualify for an unsecured line of credit. Banks generally extend a line of credit for one year. However, an unsecured line of credit is usually revolving; in other words, you can repeatedly borrow, repay, and borrow again all or part of the credit available.

In order to secure a line of credit you may have to sign short-term notes for the advances. These notes are periodically reviewed and repaid, reduced, or extended, as required.

The establishment of a line of credit protects you since normally the lender will not reduce or cancel the line of credit without good cause. However, the lender will keep an eye on your financial statements and economic and other factors that might influence your business's operations and thus change the lender's view of the appropriateness of your particular line of credit.

With a line of credit you only pay interest on money actually borrowed — not on the amount that could be. This interest may be supplemented by a small commitment fee of less than 1% on any unused portion of the line of credit.

1. Compensating balance

A business with a line of credit of any sizable amount (generally $100,000 or more) is sometimes required to keep a deposit balance with the lender. This deposit balance is usually proportional to the amount of the line of credit.

For example, it might be stipulated by the lender at 10% to 15% of the line of credit amount. This percentage might vary with the money market. Since the deposit amount is generally in an account that pays little or no interest it favors the bank and increases the effective interest rate you are paying on any money used from your line of credit.

Some banks charge service fees or ask for a higher interest rate in lieu of a compensating balance.

e. ASSIGNING ACCOUNTS RECEIVABLE

Most small businesses need cash to meet their current liability commitments, and if money is tied up in receivables a cash problem can arise. This problem is particularly so in a growing business with expanding sales.

In such a situation receivables tend to increase at the expense of cash, inventories, and even fixed assets. Unless receivables can be converted into cash in a minimum period of time the business's liquidity may be impaired. It may then run into credit problems and find its growth limited.

Attention should be paid to control of accounts receivable and collection procedures. These controls and procedures were outlined in chapter 12. In addition you might want to consider financing your accounts receivable.

Receivables can be assigned to a bank or other lender as security for a short-term loan or line of credit. The receivables can be assigned on a notification or nonnotification basis. Under a notification basis the lender notifies your customers that the accounts receivable have been pledged to the lender and directs them to make payment directly to the lender. Since this arrangement can disturb the normal relationship between you and your customers, a nonnotification basis is more common.

Under nonnotification customers continue to make payment to you. In other words you collect the receivables in the normal way, even though they are assigned. You will sign a note to the lender, and as the receivables are collected by you, you pay back the lender and retrieve your note.

Generally the lender will loan up to a certain percentage of the face value of the assigned receivables (e.g., 65%) and charge you interest and possibly a service fee.

If collections on assigned accounts are not sufficient to pay the loan, you will be responsible for the deficiency. This is a major difference from factoring. Under factoring the lender purchases your accounts receivable and takes over the loss from any uncollectible accounts (bad debts).

With accounts receivable financing you are able to secure a continuous source of operating cash without having to make long-term financing agreements. The receivables line is usually arranged for a year and renewed at the end of that time if agreed by the lender.

The main aim of accounts receivable financing is to free up funds tied up in this asset. This may put you company in a stronger position to expand sales, provide cash to pay off accounts payable to receive a discount, and improve your credit standing.

However, accounts receivable financing is not the answer to a permanent working capital deficiency but is more usefully used to cover cyclical or seasonal shortages of cash to cover current obligations as they fall due.

f. INVENTORY FINANCING

Some small businesses may have large amounts of money tied up in inventory of raw materials, work in process, or in finished goods. The cost of carrying this inventory can be as high as 30% of its value, so you might want to consider inventory financing.

Inventories are not as liquid as accounts receivable, so a bank or other lender will normally want to secure any loans made for inventory only after you have used your full ability to borrow against accounts receivable. Receivables are easier to convert into cash in the short run and do not present the same problems that certain inventories can create such as style changes, sharp price reductions, or obsolescence.

Retail and similar businesses that must carry large amounts of unsold inventory will probably experience difficulty, particularly during the start-up phase, in obtaining inventory financing because of the high failure rate of such businesses. Lenders are not anxious to accept certain types of merchandise (that they would later have difficulty disposing of if the loan were in default) as security.

In those cases, to be financible, the inventory must have a ready market and not be subject to obsolescence or perishable in any way. In other words, the inventory has to be able to be sold if you cannot meet your loan payments.

In a manufacturing or processing business, only raw material and finished goods inventory could be financed. A lender would not wish to finance work in process since it has virtually no resale value.

Despite these difficulties, inventory financing can be important to your business, particularly if you must build up inventory to meet seasonal demand for your products. The marketability of your inventory will dictate the percentage of its value that can be financed. If it is not readily marketable, this percentage could be as low as 30% to 40%. If it is extremely marketable it could be as high as 70% or 80%. The lender will probably require a warehouse receipt of trust receipt for the inventory.

g. OTHER LOANS

1. Collateral loan

You may be able to obtain a bank loan on the basis of collateral such as a chattel mortgage, stocks and bonds, cash surrender value of life insurance, and similar security.

Even with this collateral, regardless of how good it is, the lender may feel that it is no guarantee of your business's ability to repay because the lender's objective is not to cash in the collateral (since it may produce less in liquidation than the amount you owe). However, the collateral does afford the lender some security, and a collateral loan may be easier to find than a line of credit or unsecured loan for a risky business.

2. Character loan

A character loan is a short-term unsecured loan, generally restricted to an individual or his or her company with an excellent credit rating.

3. Warehouse receipt loan

If goods are stored in a warehouse, and warehouse receipts are used as security for a loan, the loan may then be used to pay off the supplier. As you sell the goods, the loan is paid off.

4. Floor plan financing

Floor planning is used as a financing vehicle by retailers of large ticket items (automobiles, appliances) that can be readily identified, usually by a serial number, and have a relatively high unit value.

In floor planning you have possession of the units and the lender retains the ownership and pays the manufacturer the cost price of the items. As you sell each item, you pay the lender the amount due on that item.

You will generally sign a note to the lender and pay interest from the time the arrangement is made until the time the item is sold. A flooring line might be renewed annually.

A trust receipt is frequently used as a legal document in floor plan financing. It acknowledges that you have received the items being floor planned, that you agree to keep them in trust for the lender, and that you promise to pay back the lender as you sell items.

5. Indirect collection financing

Indirect collection financing is also used for big ticket items sold by you to your customers on an installment paying basis. The lender will advance you 70% to 80% of the value of each item when it is sold to a customer. You repay the advance with interest as the customer pays you each installment.

6. Chattel mortgage

A chattel mortgage loan is usually for a short or intermediate term. It is secured by the movable assets (chattels) of your business that are not otherwise mortgaged or secured. The chattel mortgage provides a lien to the lender. To obtain the mortgage for your business you might have to include personal assets in the security.

The value assigned to the assets is their current liquidation value. You may be required to carry various types of insurance on the mortgaged chattels. The security is released or discharged to you when the loan is repaid.

7. Floating charge debenture

A floating charge debenture is again a short- or intermediate-term loan where the loan is secured by a general claim on the total equity of the business. A floating charge debenture (unlike a chattel mortgage or a commercial pledge that specifies and describes specific assets as security) does not describe specific assets. Instead, all assets are described in general terms (e.g., "inventory") and can be disposed of in the ordinary day-to-day operations of the business unless loan default occurs.

As a precaution the lender may impose certain restrictions or controls to ensure that your business's equity does not fall below what the lender deems is required to secure the loan.

A business with a floating charge debenture may still be able to obtain other short-term financing on specific assets, for example through a chattel mortgage. The lender holding a floating charge debenture ranks after the claims of other lenders whose claims are on specific assets.

18
INTERMEDIATE- AND LONG-TERM FINANCING

Most financing that is for more than one year is referred to as long-term. However, somewhere between short- and long-term financing is a need at times for intermediate-term financing for periods up to five years. Long-term financing is generally for periods from five to twenty-five years.

a. INTERMEDIATE-TERM FINANCING

When considering an intermediate-term loan, lending companies rely on indications of your business's profitability and ability to repay. These indications are provided by income statement and cash flow forecasts for the next several years, as well as historic income statements that indicate your forecasts are reasonable and not made on the basis of overestimated sales and underestimated expenses.

1. Term loans

A common way to obtain intermediate-term financing is through term loans. Term loans are usually repaid in regular installments of principal and interest over the life of the loan, which is usually less than the life of the assets for which financing is required. They can vary in length from one to five years.

The interest rate on term loans is usually a percentage point or more higher than that for a short-term loan made to the same borrower. The periodic payments on term loans can be geared to the business's cash flow ability to repay. In some cases only the interest portion of such loans is payable in the first year or two. Payments could be made monthly, quarterly, semiannually, or annually. Payments are calculated so that the debt is repaid (amortized) by a specific date.

Interest rates may also be negotiable. As long as you adhere to the terms of the loan, you can generally be assured that no payments other than the regular installment ones will be required before the due date of the loan. If the periodic payments do not completely amortize the debt by the maturity date, the final payment will be larger than the previous periodic payments. This larger, final payment is known as a "balloon" payment. Term loan sometimes allow early repayment without penalty.

Most term loans are offered only to companies with profit histories whose current or projected financial statements demonstrate an ability to repay. The term loan usually requires a written loan agreement that, among other things, might limit your company's other debts, owner salaries, and dividend payments. In addition, the agreement may require that a stipulated percentage of company profits must be used to increase repayment installments on the loan, otherwise the loan may be considered in default. Compensating balances are also frequently required.

Term loans also have an advantage in that they develop a lender/borrower relationship over a number of years that can be useful in future financial matters, including advice from the lender concerning preferential future financing arrangements that you could make.

Sometimes personal term loans (in addition to business loans) are available to help finance your initial equity investment in the business. However, this can be risky since the total interest cost on all loans (since little or none of the start up money is your own) can be crippling to the company's working capital.

2. Installment financing

Installment financing could be used to finance the purchase of equipment of various kinds, including automotive equipment, and fixtures (such as counters, shelves, and display cases) where term loans are unavailable.

By using an equipment loan you can retain precious working capital. Lenders will generally finance from 60% to 80% of the equipment's value; the balance after your down payment.

Although some furniture and equipment sales companies may finance this way directly, others will sell to a financing company that, in turn, will do the installment financing. Many supply companies will act as an intermediary between you and the finance company to coordinate the arrangement. In other cases you may have to shop around to arrange your own installment financing.

Since the assets being financed generally have a life averaging five to ten years, and since the financing agency runs a relatively high risk because of the very low value of second-hand furniture and equipment (and thus its low value as collateral), the length of life of such financing is usually from three to seven years with repayments of principal and interest made monthly.

There is usually a sizable down payment on such arrangements (from 20% to 30%), and the interest rate is generally much higher than with term loans; it could run as much as five or six points over prime.

Installment loans of this type are generally secured by a chattel mortgage (a lien on the assets financed), which can be registered and which permits the seller or lending company to sell the liened assets if the installment payments are in default. Alternatively, the lender's security could be a conditional sales contract, whereby the seller or lender retains title to the assets until you have satisfied all the terms of the contract.

A cyclical or seasonal business (such as a construction company or a motel) might have difficulty obtaining an installment loan since a current ratio of 2 to 1 or higher is important, particularly if the business has fluctuating earnings.

The installment loan agreement also usually binds you to maintaining working capital at an agreed-upon level and to obtaining lender approval before making any other capital expenditure for your business over a specified limit. It might also limit the amount that can be paid in salaries and bonuses and require that assets be kept free of encumbrances. Finally, the agreement might require that a proportion of profits be applied to loan repayments above and beyond the amount stipulated in your note payable securing the loan.

Installment financing does not have to be limited to new equipment. It can also be used to finance used equipment whose original financing has been paid off. In such cases as much as 60% of the equipment's present appraised value may be raised in cash to be repaid in monthly installments over the remaining term of the equipment's useful life.

b. LONG-TERM FINANCING

Where long-term debt is required it will probably be in the form of a mortgage, which is a grant, by the borrower to a creditor or lender, of preference or priority in a particular asset. This asset is usually some type of real estate.

When loans are secured by a mortgage the value of the real estate that is the security is not always the only factor considered. Lenders know, from experience, that there is some risk involved in making mortgage loans on certain types of buildings, particularly on special purpose ones such as a manufacturing plant or a motel that cannot easily be adapted to any other use.

For this reason, other than in the case of a new business, the track record of the borrower over a number of years and the probability of being able to repay the debt as indicated by past financial statements is often given as much weight as the value of the property mortgaged.

If the borrower is in default (e.g., for nonpayment of interest and/or principal owing), the creditor holding the mortgage is entitled to force the sale of the specific asset or assets pledged as security. Proceeds of the sale would go to the holder of the first mortgage before any other creditors would receive anything.

If another creditor had a mortgage on the same asset or assets, he or she would be classified as a second mortgage holder, and would rank below the first mortgage holder but above a third mortgage holder (if one existed) or other creditors of the borrower in default. The legal procedure by which the first mortgage holder can force the sale is called foreclosure.

In the business world, first mortgage lenders are generally organizations that have collected savings from many individual investors or lenders. The organization, acting as an intermediary, combines these savings and lends them in lump sums. Such organizations are insurance companies, pension companies, real estate investment trusts, commercial and mortgage banks, and even trust companies and credit unions.

1. Feasibility studies and other requirements

Before lending money, these organizations would consider factors such as your past business experience. If you had a proven record of five years or more of successful experience you would more likely be able to obtain funds at a reasonable rate than would a novice.

Lenders are also concerned about the amount of equity invested by you and other owners. This equity usually takes the form of a direct cash investment or purchase of shares if the company is incorporated. Without such equity investment, the mortgage lender is taking a very high-risk position.

Generally, such equity needs to be a minimum of 25% to 30% of total company financing.

A prospective lender would also be concerned that proper accounting procedures, particularly for cost control, will be instituted. Lenders frequently require audited financial statements at least yearly but sometimes more frequently. This allows them to read possible danger signs before it is too late.

Some lenders carry out on-site inspections of properties in which they have mortgaged investments to ensure that the property is not run down and that it is being maintained adequately. This ensures that their investment is better protected. In some cases the mortgage investor may stipulate a percentage of annual revenue that must be spent on property maintenance.

2. Loan terms

Generally, first mortgages can be obtained for up to 70% or 75% of the appraised value of the land and building offered as security for the loan. If the land is leased, then the mortgage would usually be obtainable only on the appraised value of the building.

Loan terms usually range between 20 and 25 years. However, the term could be as short as 10 years.

Repayment of loans is generally made in equal monthly payments of principal and interest. These payments are calculated so that, at the stated interest rate, the regular payments will completely amortize (pay off) the mortgage by the end of its life. Sometimes the payments are calculated so that, during the early years, interest only is paid (with no reduction in principal).

3. Early prepayment

Most first mortgage loans do not permit any early prepayment for at least the first several years. Thus you are locked in for that period and cannot benefit if interest rates decline.

Where prepayment is allowed, the lender may impose a penalty — usually a percentage of the balance still owing, which may decline as time goes by. You might be prepared to pay such a penalty. For example, if the initial mortgage carried an 18% interest rate, and current rates had declined to 14%, you might be able to negotiate a new loan with a new lender and use part of the proceeds to pay off the remaining balance of the initial mortgage plus penalty. The penalty imposition may be more than offset by the interest reduction over the term of the new mortgage.

Since circumstances in each case will differ, each decision about long-term mortgage refinancing must be made on its own merits.

4. Call provision

Just as you may be permitted early repayment opportunities to benefit from changed general market interest rates, so too the lender is usually protected. Most mortgage agreements have a call provision in them that allows the lender, after a stated number of years, to ask for complete repayment of the mortgage. The lender and borrower then renegotiate a new mortgage at a new interest rate for a further stipulated period of time. A lender would probably call a loan if interest rates had increased since the original mortgage agreement was signed.

There is also an increasing trend toward variable interest rate mortgages where the interest rate, depending on market conditions, can be changed up or down by the lender as frequently as monthly.

5. Other compensation

Some lenders also require additional compensation such as a fee, discount, or bonus. For example, a $10,000 bonus on a $250,000 mortgage would mean you receive only $240,000 but must pay back principal and interest on the $250,000. Such front-end "loads" obviously raise the effective interest rate.

Other lenders may ask for an equity participation. This equity participation increases the lender's return on his investment and, at the same time, dilutes your return on investment. Equity might take the form of a percentage of annual revenue or an investment in common shares.

6. Joint venture

In some cases the lender might enter into a joint venture agreement with you. Such an agreement might provide you with some equity funds (while giving up part of equity control) as well as mortgage funds.

In other cases the mortgage investor might supply 100% of the total project cost for which he or she receives a substantial equity position. This might significantly reduce your capital outlay and at the same time reduce your risk, control, and potential future income.

7. Equipment and fixture

Most long-term mortgage lenders will not normally finance any portion of the equipment and fixtures. The prime reason is that mortgage lenders are in the long-term loan business, and furniture and equipment have a relatively short-term life.

However, despite this, they will sometimes attempt to obtain a first mortgage on these chattels (in addition to the long-term mortgage on the assets that they have financed). In this way, if the first mortgage lender has to foreclose, he or she is sure that the equipment and fixtures will not be removed and that the business can continue to operate.

8. Second mortgages

Second mortgages are also used for financing land and building. A second mortgage lender would take a second lien on the property mortgaged. The loan amount is generally limited to 5% to 15% of the appraised value of the property, and loan terms usually range from 5 to 15 years.

Second mortgage interest rates are generally three to four points above first mortgage rates because of the additional risk involved. Repayments are made by you over the life of the loan by way of equal monthly installments of principal and interest.

An excessive second mortgage can be risky to both you and the lender because of potential cash flow problems if the business is not successful.

9. Refinancing

If your property already has a mortgage on it that has been running for some years, you might want to consider refinancing to raise required funds.

By refinancing, a new mortgage is written based on the present value of the property. You will receive in cash the difference between the old and the new mortgage and make your loan payments on the new mortgage. Since these payments will likely be higher than the previous ones, you must be sure that the increased borrowing is used to generate additional long-run profits. It is extremely risky to remortgage your property to raise working capital — and lenders are unlikely to take that risk.

19
SOURCES OF FUNDING

Financing is available from a wide selection of commercial sources. It is also available from government sources (to be discussed later).

The wise loan shopper should realize that commercial lenders (the ones in business primarily for a profit) consider risk the most important factor when establishing interest rates, whereas the main objective of government agencies is to aid small businesses. Because of this their funds are in limited supply.

You must shop around to locate the type of loan that suits your business's needs and then match that with the appropriate source, keeping the interest rate in mind but realizing that, as a small business, you often have little choice. Some of the major sources of financing are discussed below.

a. BANKS

The most visible and numerous lenders are the commercial banks. They are also the most conservative. It is said that they will do their best to lend you an umbrella, but if it rains demand that you return it immediately.

Banks probably provide about 80% of all business loans. Although they often want plenty of security and proof of cash flow and ability to repay, they are also influenced by a business's profitability, management expertise, and track records.

Banks require a certain amount of owner equity in the business — for example, 25% — before they will consider advancing funds. These funds will be primarily for working capital purposes (financing inventory and accounts receivable), or in the form of short- or medium-term loans for capital purchases.

Banks also offer a line of credit. This line could be up to 65% or 70% of all accounts receivable not over 60 days old, 40% to 45% of inventory value, or 35% to 40% of the appraised value of fixed assets (although the last is rare).

Their security could be on real or personal property, inventory of any kind, or even the equipment used in the manufacturing or processing of goods.

The amounts that can be borrowed from banks, as well as their interest rates, can be negotiated. Usually the higher the amount to be borrowed, given adequate security, the lower the rate. The rate will usually be about three to four points over prime for the small business operator.

With banks it is sometimes preferable to go to the local main office rather than to a branch. Your own branch office may service the loan, but if the loan is of any size, the main office will have to approve it anyway. In some cases the local main office may itself have to have approval from the regional head office.

Since banks are very conservative lenders, they will check your credit standing through trade creditors, other banks you may have done business with, and credit bureaus. They also put great emphasis on your financial statements (balance sheet and income statement), and prefer audited ones.

If you do borrow from a bank after the bank has checked you out, you can be sure that your business appears to be on fairly solid footing. However, remember that banks do make mistakes!

b. COMMERCIAL FINANCE COMPANIES

A new, or rapidly expanding, small business may find a commercial bank unwilling to lend money because it lacks a track record, there is a large amount of financing required, or there is a high debt to equity ratio. An established business may run into the same kind of problems with commercial banks because of the banks' conservatism.

In such cases you may need to seek out commercial finance companies that offer many of the services offered by commercial banks. Commercial finance companies, like banks, are concerned with your ability to repay a loan, but they are more likely to rely on your business's collateral quality than track record or forecast profits and cash flow. They may also be more flexible than commercial banks.

Commercial finance companies offer both accounts receivable and inventory financing, as well as term loans up to five years secured by new equipment. They may also finance used equipment to the extent that equity in fully owned equipment can be used instead of a cash down payment on new equipment purchases. Sometimes they offer term loans up to 10 years secured by commercial or industrial real estate, including both first and second mortgage refinancing.

Some more venturesome finance companies have been known to provide partially or totally unsecured long-term loans of from two to ten years based on their assessment of a company's profitability and cash flow rather than on collateral.

Commercial finance companies are also involved in equipment leasing and factoring, as well as sale and leaseback of equipment — financial investments that a commercial bank would seldom, if ever, be involved in.

However, since commercial finance companies run higher risks than banks, and because they frequently borrow some of the money they lend from those banks, their interest rates are usually higher.

c. SAVINGS AND LOAN ASSOCIATIONS

Savings and loan associations are primarily in the commercial, industrial, and personal real estate financing business. They will generally make mortgages available for as little as $10,000, advancing up to 75% or 80% of the property value and allowing repayment periods for as long as 25 years. Interest rates vary as the mortgage market varies, and their interest rates are competitive with banks, commercial finance companies, and life insurance companies.

They will deal with both customers and noncustomers but are concerned with the appraised value of the property, its marketability, and location. As is true of commercial banks they dislike very specialized types of manufacturing business and rely heavily on the borrower's personal and business financial statements and proof of ability to pay.

d. FACTORS

A factor is a company that evaluates the credit and collection potential of the accounts receivable of a business and, if considered satisfactory, takes over those accounts and assumes responsibility for collection. If you factor your accounts, you are paid cash by the factor company while your customers continue to benefit from the normal credit terms that you allow.

Factors do not make loans. They simply purchase your accounts for their perceived value, usually advancing up to 80% of their worth, and pay you the remainder (less their factor fee and interest charges) when they collect from your customers.

Generally speaking they deal in short-term accounts receivable of 30 to 90 days and do not handle long-term installment sales. They may at times extend receivable time to six months and extend medium-term loans to regular customers and secure these loans with warehouse receipts or similar collateral.

If a factor assumes your accounts receivable without recourse, this means that it will absorb any bad debt losses and assume the risk, although the factor may hold back from payment to you when a purchaser refuses to pay for faulty merchandise or under similar circumstances.

The factor's fee varies from 1% to 2% of the invoice plus interest on the money advanced to you. The cost is generally higher than either bank or commercial finance company rates for financing your own receivables.

Factors look for a reputable business operator who has reliable customers who pay promptly. In addition they do not like to have receivables concentrated in one or two large accounts. They also like to be sure you honor warranties, service sales, and handle customer complaints satisfactorily.

e. LIFE INSURANCE COMPANIES

Life insurance companies can sometimes be a useful source of cash when you borrow on your policy. In addition, life insurance companies also offer commercial mortgages (even if you are not a policy holder) as well as unsecured term loans to what they consider safe businesses.

1. Life insurance policies

Before a life insurance policy can be used to raise cash, it must generally have been in effect for two years at which point you may borrow up to 95% of its cash value for an indeterminate period. Interest is normally charged yearly but may be deferred indefinitely as long as you continue to regularly pay your insurance premiums. However, recognize that your loan erodes the dollar value of the insurance policy and your coverage will only be the amount you have not borrowed.

Since policy loans are based on paid-in cash, and thus require little risk from the insurance company, they often provide loans at interest rates less than the banks' prime rate.

2. Mortgages

For long-term mortgage loans, life insurance companies are generally interested in a minimum period of 15 years or more. Because of this their interest rates have been traditionally lower than other sources. They may also want an option to buy shares in companies to which they lend money. Principal and interest payments are generally payable monthly, as is typical of most mortgages.

Life insurance mortgage loans are frequently handled through independent loan agents such as mortgage bankers. The mortgage loan banker, for a loan service fee, acts as the intermediary between you and the insurance company. Up to 75% of the appraised value of the property can be borrowed this way.

f. CONSUMER FINANCE COMPANIES

When other sources of debt financing are unavailable, many small business owners have used consumer finance companies on a personal loan basis.

Consumer or personal finance companies can provide loans as high as or higher than $25,000 that can be used to finance a small business. Smaller loans of $5,000 to $10,000 may be secured by personal assets (such as a car).

In the case of loans over $10,000, your home is the security, even if it is already mortgaged, since the loan company will take out a second mortgage on the equity balance beyond the first mortgage. Payment periods vary from a few months up to a few years.

Some consumer finance companies offer unsecured or signature loans in addition to their secured loans. These loans are normally only made to customers with excellent credit ratings.

Consumer finance companies base their loans on the credit worthiness of the individual and the liquidation value of security offered. Applicants are usually required to supply current and past personal credit and other financial data. If your business is the cash source for loan repayment, you will have to provide cash flow statements to demonstrate ability to repay.

Consumer loan companies usually take care of those who are unable to obtain bank or similar credit. Therefore, they are high risk lenders and their interest rates are considerably higher than bank rates for a similar loan.

g. CREDIT UNIONS

Credit unions are becoming a popular source of funds for small businesses. To obtain funds you must be a member and leave on deposit with them in a share account a nominal amount of $25 or $30 that cannot be withdrawn during the term of the loan.

Although short-term loans are preferred, credit unions will make longer loans secured by a real property mortgage. Their rates are competitive with those of commercial banks.

h. VENTURE CAPITAL

There are a number of investment organizations known as venture capital companies that specialize in funding small business. The term small, in this case, does not mean really small. Generally, venture capitalists are interested in making loans only in the $100,000 to $500,000 range for any single venture.

Since these investment companies are more interested in financing ongoing companies, rather than brand new ventures, they might well be interested in helping you with the purchase of a successful ongoing business, particularly if you have plans to expand it.

Venture capital is available from these companies in both debt and equity form although it is more common for them to take an equity position (common or preferred shares) since that allows them to participate more easily in the extra profits from the growth of your company.

Under normal circumstances, despite their equity position, venture capitalists are not interested in involvement in the day-to-day operations of your business unless it is having difficulty meeting its obligations. In that case they may well seek a say in management. However, they might nevertheless seek controls to safeguard their investment. These controls might include the right to veto large capital expenditures, to approve management salaries, to have the final decision on loans over and above normal day-to-day financing, and similar matters. Decisions affecting the general financial situation of your company are very important to the venture capitalist.

Normally they would look for a 20% a year compound rate of growth in your profits and a good likelihood of capital gain on their share holdings in your company by selling their shares in a few years so they can invest the proceeds in new investments. Sometimes this divestment of their shares takes place progressively as your company matures.

Extracting funds from venture capitalists is not easy. They receive many more applications from people than they can ever fund. You will have to prepare a well-documented financial plan when approaching a venture capital company.

Some venture capital companies are affiliated with banks and similar financial institutions, insurance companies, and some large corporations looking for diversification. Other venture capitalists are groups of wealthy individuals or families and private groups of investors who have pooled their resources to seek out healthy investments.

Selling common stock to venture capital companies can be an expensive form of financing. If your business prospers through your hard work, it is sometimes frustrating to see much of the reward going to others through a financial commitment made earlier. Before approaching a venture capital company you should explore all other avenues of financing that do not mean giving up an equity share.

1. Requirements

Management is the key to the success of any small business, regardless of the product or service it sells. Therefore, the quality of your management is a major factor in attracting favorable attention from venture capitalists. They are also looking for investments in businesses in industries that are growing rapidly.

Venture capital investors are attracted to a better product or service — one that has a competitive advantage. They would be keenly interested in a new idea or product, supported by market and competition analysis, showing that it has a good chance of success.

Finally, cash flow is critical. Many small business operators have their priorities back to front ranking their objectives as growth first, profits second, and cash flow third. If the business grows faster than the cash flow it will soon run out of cash and be unable to pay its debts. The venture capital investor is looking for the business owner who can balance growth in sales with profits and cash flow and understands the importance of cash flow to allow the company to expand using internally generated financing.

2. Suppliers

One source of venture capital, apart from friends and relatives on the one hand and the major venture investment companies on the other hand, is any of the major suppliers of the product you are dealing with. This is particularly true if you are in the wholesale or retail business.

By providing financing for you your supplier may be able to obtain a larger market share and provide your venture capital for either start-up or expansion costs. This type of venture financing can sometimes be obtained at little or no cost since the supplier's return will come through increased sales to you.

Your bank manager or loan officer should be able to direct you to venture capital companies in your area.

i. SMALL BUSINESS ADMINISTRATION (U.S.)

If all else fails, you might want to consider the Small Business Administration (SBA) in the United States. The SBA was created in 1953 by the federal government to succeed several predecessor agencies responsible for assisting entrepreneurs. Its functions include, among others, finance and investment.

The SBA is organized into 10 regions, each subdivided to provide services in many areas. As the lender of final resort, the SBA tries not to compete with or replace the private banking system but to supplement it.

SBA guidelines defining who qualifies for small business assistance vary, depending on the general classification of the enterprise. Currently, the eligibility of businesses is measured by sales volume or revenue. For example, the upper limit varies from $3.5 to $14.5 million per year depending on the nature of the business for retail/service businesses.

Loans made by SBA generally mature in 10 years or less for fixtures and equipment and are repaid in equal monthly installments of principal and interest, although this time period may be extended to 25 years where the purchase of land and/or a building are concerned. Working capital loans can be made for periods up to seven years. Regardless of the loan term, the loan may be repaid at any time prior to maturity without penalty.

There are three types of loans available from the SBA: guaranteed loans, immediate participation loans, and direct loans.

1.   Guaranteed loans

Since the philosophy of the SBA is that the private banking industry is the basic mechanism for the distribution of debt financing to small business, loans are made to a business by a bank or similar lending institution, but at a reduced risk because the SBA guarantees to pay part of any loss the lending bank might suffer. Under the guaranteed loan arrangement, up to 90% of a loan or $500,000 may be guaranteed, whichever is less.

The interest rate charged by a bank for a guaranteed loan may not exceed the prime rate by more than $2\frac{1}{4}$% for loans of less than seven years maturity, and the prime rate plus $2\frac{3}{4}$% for loans of over seven years. The actual interest rate is negotiable, but the majority of loans tend to be near the high end of the range. In rare cases it may be possible to borrow at or even below the prime rate. This could occur in a chain franchise operation because of the financial strength of the franchisor.

2.   Immediate participation loans

In cases where a guaranteed loan cannot be arranged, an immediate participation loan may be available. With this type of loan, the SBA and the bank each provide a portion of the loan. For example, the bank may lend the major share of the funds required and be permitted to charge interest up to $2\frac{3}{4}$% over prime.

This interest rate is negotiable and could even be a fluctuating rate as market conditions change. The balance of the loan is from the SBA and its interest cost is based on the government's cost of funds, but by law cannot exceed a rate that is 1% less than the maximum rate banks are allowed to charge on guaranteed SBA loans. The SBA's share of an immediate participation loan may not exceed $150,000.

3. Direct loans

Direct loans are generally arranged at interest rates considerably less than those on SBA-sponsored bank loans. Direct loans may not exceed $150,000 without special approval, and in no case can they exceed the maximum limit of $350,000 established by law.

Since direct loans are derived from a limited pool of funds, the availability is restricted. In the majority of cases, application for a direct loan is made only after the prospective borrower has demonstrated that credit is not otherwise available.

Since the SBA's regulations do change from time to time, you should verify current conditions by contacting the nearest branch of the SBA (listed in your telephone directory under U.S. Government) or write to —

Small Business Administration
Washington, DC 20416

j. FEDERAL BUSINESS DEVELOPMENT BANK (CANADA)

In Canada you should also be aware of the Federal Business Development Bank, or FBDB. This lender is sometimes referred to as the lender of last resort. It was established by the government especially to help those companies that could not obtain financing elsewhere on reasonable terms and conditions.

If your funding application has been turned down by other financial institutions, you may apply to the FBDB.

To obtain FBDB financing the amount of your investment in the business must generally be sufficient to ensure that you are committed to it and that the business may have a reasonable expectation of success.

FBDB financing is available by means of loans, loan guarantees, equity financing, venture financing (a combination of loan and equity), or by any combination of these methods, in whatever way best suits the particular needs of your business. If loans are involved, they are usually at interest rates in line with those of other banks. If equity is involved, the FBDB generally takes a minority interest and is prepared to have you buy back its equity on suitable terms when the business is able to do this.

Most of the FBDB's customers use funds to acquire land, buildings, or equipment, although it is possible to use those funds to provide a healthy working capital for the business or for major plant overhauls, expansion projects, change of ownership, bridge or interim financing, as well as a wide variety of other needs. The amount that can be borrowed for a specific purpose depends on your ability to satisfy the bank's general requirements and repayment conditions are usually tied to your cash flow.

Also, once you have arranged financing from the FBDB, there is nothing to prevent you from returning and requesting further funding at a later date. If you wish to pursue this, contact your local branch of the FBDB, or write to —

Federal Business Development Bank
800 Victoria Square
Tour de la Place — Victoria
P.O. Box 335
Montreal, Quebec
H4Z 1L4

20
FINANCIAL PLAN

The size of a business has a bearing on the amount of financing it needs. Generally, the smaller the business the less its financial requirements. As a business grows, so will its financial needs and the variety of possible reasons for needing funding.

a. REASONS FOR FINANCING

There are a number of different reasons why companies need money, such as to start up a new business, to provide working capital, to handle a seasonal peak, to purchase new equipment and facilities, to finance remodeling, to finance growth of your company, and to enlarge or add to your premises.

1. Starting a new business

To start a new business will require a different amount of financing depending on the type of business, whether premises can be rented or must be built or purchased, the amount of start-up inventory that must be purchased, and the amount of working capital required until cash can be generated from sales.

A new business has to be fairly precise in its projections since that will show, among other things, whether or not cash will be generated to repay any loans made to start up the business.

The larger the business, and the more that has to be borrowed, the more detailed the financial plan will have to be, since lenders are not going to be sympathetic to a request for funding supported by figures scratched out on the back of an envelope.

Businesses with the highest start-up costs are generally those requiring a manufacturing process, high technology, and sophisticated production systems. These require specific types or sizes of buildings and expensive equipment and machinery. A retail business, on the other hand, may require much less initial investment, particularly if it is in leased premises. However, if you own the land, construct a building, and invest heavily in equipment, fixtures, and inventory, the start-up costs can also be quite high. A service business (e.g., barber shop, real estate company, employment agency,) may require little or no initial investment and, in some cases, can be operated out of a home.

If the business can be started with little or no borrowed money then, when it is proved successful, financing from outside sources will be easier and the advantages of leverage can be used.

2. Working capital requirements

Both new and ongoing businesses need money for working capital for purchasing inventory, carrying receivables, and similar ongoing situations. Working capital has been discussed in some detail in earlier chapters, as have methods for financing current assets such as accounts receivable and inventory.

3. Seasonal peak

Funding required for a seasonal or cyclical business usually involves working capital accounts. In other words, a business borrows short-term funds prior to the production/sales peak period and repays later when the increased inventory has been converted into receivables and then into cash. These cyclical or seasonal requirements for peak periods can best be forecast using cash budgeting (see chapter 12).

One of the risks with seasonal financing is that inventory will not sell as well as predicted. This may leave a business with an unsold inventory and an inability to repay loans.

4. New equipment and/or facilities

When a business needs to replace old equipment or add to its present equipment it often has to borrow money, or borrow at least part of it. This type of cash requirement is of an intermediate-term type, and you should not use working capital funds for that.

5. Remodeling

Remodeling can be a major occasion for financial borrowing. Remodeling should occur only if it will also improve sales. After remodeling, costs will probably also increase but that increase should be less than the increase in sales.

6. Sales growth

If your business is expanding rapidly through sales growth, you may need funds to carry a larger inventory, increase production, add employees to your payroll, and even add equipment.

Frequently the funding for this type of expansion cannot be financed from internal operations and money of various types may be required. This money could come from short-term or intermediate-term sources.

Under rapid growth, a seasonal business may face as many problems as a new business starting up, so it is important that rapid growth be anticipated and a detailed financing plan be prepared well in advance so that appropriate funding can be arranged.

7. Enlarging or adding to premises

If you are adding to or enlarging your premises, it is likely that you will have to provide much of the money for this from outside lenders. This type of funding is long-term and projections of increased profits and cash flow must show that you can afford to pay back both interest and principal on this type of borrowing.

b. FINANCIAL PLANNING

Financial planning is not something that happens only intermittently. Although major investments, such as starting a new business or expanding your premises, do not occur regularly, other parts of financing, such as funding working capital, expanding sales, and anticipating seasonal variations, are an ongoing process.

For example, every well-managed business prepares a budget or financial plan at least once a year. This budget aids you in operating your business in the coming year by forcing you to appraise your business to ensure that all of its aspects are evaluated for the next 12 months. It may even show you that you must also prepare a financial plan to obtain financing for an anticipated change in your business.

The first question you must ask when seeking financing is why you need it. The reasons will probably be found in the categories discussed earlier. The next step is to determine how much money is needed since that is the first question that any potential lender is going to ask you.

The third step is to decide how any borrowed money is going to be repaid. Regardless of whether you approach friends, a local banker, or a major investment company, they will want some statement, and preferably documentation, about how the money can be paid back out of profits and cash flow, and over what period of time.

In particular, if money is in short supply and interest rates high, and the reason for seeking financing can be deferred, then that is a decision you might want to make. You must be sure that you can afford the cost of any borrowed money. In other words, the income it generates must exceed expenses, and cash flow must be adequate to pay back any loan with interest. You must be confident about that before making the final commitment to borrow money.

1. What's involved in financing?

Knowing what's involved in securing financing can give you a distinct advantage. The most important fact to remember is that you are in competition with other people and other businesses for the same money.

It is often said that there is a shortage of funds for financing small businesses. However, what is more often the case is that many small business planners, owners, or operators are unfamiliar with the range of sources of funds and financial services available to them.

Another common complaint is that banks and other financial institutions turn down funding requests by insisting on 100% guarantees of the success of the business venture when the real reason is that they were just not provided with sufficient documented information to make a positive decision. Therefore, being prepared, understanding the procedures involved, and having familiarity with the different types of financing available are the first steps in demonstrating good management of a financial proposal.

2. Competition among lenders

You should also understand that banks and other financial institutions are no different than you: they are in competition with each other in the same way you are with your competitors. Banks make money by lending money out at a profit. If they don't lend money, they don't make that profit. However, for business to be profitable to the bank, the bank has to assess the risk in lending its money.

In the business of borrowing money, the words risk and interest are closely connected. Risk is the degree of danger the lender has in losing funds loaned to you. Interest is what you pay a lender for the use of borrowed funds. Normally, the higher the risk, the higher the interest rate.

Decisions made by bankers are based on their judgment of the viability of your proposal. This judgment follows no secret formulas (since banks do make errors in lending money that they cannot collect). However, bankers do use certain basic information to determine risk and make decisions. This basic information is usually derived from data provided in your loan application.

c. PREPARING THE PAPERWORK

The style and content of a loan application are of major importance when asking for a loan. To make the best impression on those approached for funding, it is critical to have all the facts properly documented. Regardless of the type of loan, the information required by the lender will be basically the same.

The lender will want to know who you are, what your plans are, and what these plans will do for the business. The preparation of this information in answer to the lender's questions, and the analysis that backs it up, is quite simple. A systematized approach to preparing this information for a lender you have not previously dealt with should include —

(a) Resume of the owner

(b) Personal financial information

(c) References

(d) Products and/or services

(e) Financial statements

(f) Security offered

(g) Insurance policies

(h) Credit rating

(i) Formal loan plan layout

(j) Any other considerations

1. Resume of the owner

The lender will want to know something about you (and any other owners) such as your education and experience (or lack of it) and how this will be valuable to the business.

The lender will want to be assured of your managerial skills. A past track record demonstrating ability in matters such as production, marketing, financing, and similar areas and how these can be related to the business you are in are some determining factors in assessing your management ability. In essence the lender needs this information to size up your character (as well as that of any other partners or shareholders in the business), honesty, reliability, trustworthiness, responsibility, willingness to work, and wise use of any borrowed funds.

The lender can then compare, from his or her own experience in lending money to other businesses, the relative strengths of your case.

2. Personal financial information

If you do not have a previous business track record the lender will probably need personal financial information about you and the other owners. This information will show the lender what other financial support you can fall back on if the business runs into difficulty and requires further owner investment. A personal financial information form is illustrated in Sample #31.

3. References

You will probably need to provide references, both personal and business. If you have dealt with other banks previously, references from them can be helpful, including details of any previous or present loans outstanding with those banks. The names of your accountant and lawyer are also useful for references.

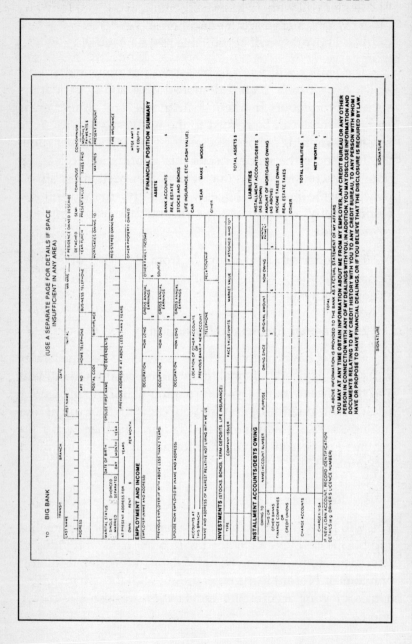

4. Products and/or services

The lender will want some details about the products and services of your company. This will include information concerning sales trends of the products, their prices, their quality in comparison with competitors, and any proposed change in the product mix and the effect of that on profits.

The lender is concerned with matters such as the acceptability of your business's products, their diversity, their competitiveness, and the possible problems of borrowed money going into risky new products.

When considering future prospects, the bank might want to consider the impact of environmental and/or technological change on your business. Such factors as the availability of labor (if it is a labor-intensive business), consistency of supply of required raw materials, and the adequacy of the present building and equipment to meet your projected future sales would be of concern to the lender.

An assessment of your market, and potential market share could be included at this point. Finally, don't be reticent about including the names of your nearest competitors.

5. Financial statement

Financial statement projections will be required for the next 12 months with detailed calculations showing, in particular, how total annual revenue is calculated and what the operating costs are projected to be. Forecast cash flow projections, month by month for the next year, will also be required.

You will need to provide past financial statements going back at least three years if you have been in business that long. These financial statements would include income statement, balance sheets, and possible cash flow statements.

In other words, the lender is interested in how your business is doing, its direction and possible growth and, most important, its ability to repay any loans from cash flow. In particular, the lender will be looking for potential problems indicated by your financial statement. These problems could be matters such as overdue receivables, overvalued inventory, too high inventory in relation to sales, large loans to owners, too high a dividend payout or owner cash withdrawals, a serious possible decline in sales in poor economic times, or too much investment in fixed assets in relation to sales.

The amount of your investment or equity in the business is important. Banks and other lending institutions do not finance 100% of the financial needs of a business. You have to put some of your own money in, as much as 25% of the total cash required.

You might like to show how the required money is going to be used, and the various sources of funding. A very simple plan would look like this:

USE OF FUNDS

Building addition	$100,000
New equipment	23,000
Contingencies	7,000
Total	$130,000

SOURCE OF FUNDS

Bank loan	$105,000
Shareholder loan	25,000
Total	$130,000

6. Security offered

The prospective lender will want details of the security offered for any loan. This includes a description of the assets (land, building, equipment and fixtures, accounts receivable, inventory, and even firm sales contracts). If you can offer personal security (house, stocks, bonds, life insurance, and similar items), this should be listed as well. In particular, if you own the land and/or building and there has been a recent appraisal, this will be useful since it will indicate what the property is worth.

If the land and/or building are not owned, a lease agreement that you have might form the security offered. In this case, a copy of the lease agreement should be provided the lender along with a statement from the landlord showing that all rent payments already made (if any) have been made promptly. If any of your assets are currently secured against other mortgages or loans, you must provide details such as the specific assets involved, the amount originally borrowed against them, and the amount still outstanding.

The amount of security required by lenders will differ in each case. If a business is stable, mature, and has built up solid credit with a lender, the demand for security is lessened. Real estate is generally valued at 75% of its market price, equipment at 50% to 80% depending on its age, and inventory as low as 50%.

For a successful ongoing business a major item of security could be the future earnings potential of the business.

7. Insurance policies

The lender will want to know if the business is adequately insured against losses and liabilities and, in each case, who the beneficiaries are. Therefore, copies of any insurance policies should be made available to the lender.

8. Credit rating

It is important that both you and your business have a good credit rating since lenders (and even suppliers in the case of a new business) will frequently refer to that to help make a decision. You should contact your local office of a reputable credit reporting agency if you have not already established a credit rating.

213

Credit reporting agencies will require much of the information outlined above so that they can prepare a brief synopsis of your business and your personal background. This information should be freely given to ensure that they have accurate information. Any information they have about you from other sources (suppliers and lenders with whom you have done business, and from personal or business references) is available to you for your inspection.

If it is correctly documented and up-to-date, a credit report can be helpful in influencing a lender who refers to that credit agency for the current report on your credit background.

9. Formal loan plan layout

The following is an outline of a formal loan plan that you can use if required. Many financial lenders, particularly if they are familiar with your business from previous occasions, do not need this type of formal outline but are quite satisfied with the answers to the questions discussed above. But there may be occasion when it is advantageous to follow or adapt the outline format shown in Sample #32.

10. Other considerations

The importance of careful preparation of all paperwork outlined above cannot be overstressed. The manner in which this information is professionally prepared and presented to a potential lender will go a long way toward ensuring that the required funds will be obtained.

In calculating projected sales and expenses, accuracy is critical. If careless errors are made in overestimating revenue or underestimating expenses (thus producing a padded profit amount), your credibility will be damaged. The chances of obtaining borrowed funds will be considerably decreased. For this reason professional help from a financial consultant or an accountant may be necessary.

SAMPLE #32
LOAN PLAN OUTLINE

A. Summary

1. Nature of your business
2. Reason for loan and amount required
3. Proposed terms of repayment
4. Amount of additional equity investment and resulting debt/equity ratio
5. Security or collateral for loan

B. Personal Information

1. Your education and business background
2. Credit references
3. Personal income tax statements for past three years
4. Personal financial statements

C. Business Information

1. Brief business story
2. Current balance sheet
3. Income statements for past several years

D. Financial Projections

1. Sales and expense projections for next 12 months, by month
2. Cash flow projections for next 12 months, by month
3. Proposed balance sheet one year hence

(Any necessary explanations should be included with these projections.)

Even though a suggested list of paperwork items has been outlined it might be a good idea to contact potential lenders, in each specific case, to determine what they would like to be presented with.

This will ensure that time is not needlessly spent putting together a report that is far more than a lender is interested in or, alternatively, a report that fails to include some specific item that the lender does want.

When seeking financing it is a good idea to make appointments in a businesslike way with each potential lender. That is more likely to portray the image of a professional business operator than by just simply walking in the door and asking for money.

For more information, you might want to refer to *Preparing a Successful Business Plan*, another title in the Self-Counsel Series.

d. LENDING DECISIONS

When you are applying for funds there are two possibilities: the funding will be approved or denied.

1. Funding approved

If a request for financing is approved, find out everything you need to know about the conditions, terms, payment methods, interest rates, security requirements, and if there are any front-end charges or fees to be paid. No commitment to accept the financing should be made until all this information is provided and understood and its implications considered.

If you are told that financing will be approved if certain other conditions are met, determine if these conditions are severe enough to restrict the operating standards you desire. Will the conditions commit you to more than was intended, or are they normal financing requirements that were simply overlooked?

Once a final commitment is made, it is a good idea to provide the lender with copies of future financial statements. Frequently this will be one of the requirements for obtaining funding. Even if it is not, it will provide the lender with progress reports about the business and will be helpful to the lender in processing future applications for further financing.

2. Funding denied

If a request for financing is not approved, find out why. Use the lender's experience to advantage. He or she will have a reason for not providing the financing. Lenders handle many requests for financing and have experience in the financial aspects (even if they do not have direct management experience) of many businesses.

For example, the lender might be able to see that your business will run into a shortage of working capital with the financial plan proposed. A shortage of working capital is one of the common reasons for failure of many small businesses. If a business is in trouble because of this, it is often difficult to obtain additional working capital assistance.

It is far preferable to ask for additional funds to strengthen working capital at the outset, and a potential lender may well be able to point this out as a possible problem with your proposed financing plan.

If there is something else wrong with the financing proposal, see if it can be corrected and then reapply. If not, use this knowledge when approaching other potential lenders, or on future occasions when seeking funds.

If you have enjoyed this book and would like to receive a free catalogue of all Self-Counsel titles, please write to the appropriate address below:

Self-Counsel Press
1481 Charlotte Road
North Vancouver, B.C.
V7J 1H1

Self-Counsel Press
1704 N. State Street
Bellingham, Washington
98225